**WEST WYANDOTTE
KANSAS CITY KANSAS
PUBLIC LIBRARY
DATE:**

DEC 2 2008035

perfect

Perfect Readings for Weddings

Jonathan Law was born in Westonzoyland, Somerset, in 1961 and obtained his degree in English from Oxford University. Since 1989 he has worked as an editor at Market House Books, where he has contributed to numerous dictionaries, encyclopedias, and other reference works. He is the editor or co-editor of *European Culture: A Contemporary Companion* (1993), *The Cassell Companion to Cinema* (1995), *Who's Who in the Twentieth Century* (1999), *The Macmillan Dictionary of Contemporary Phrase and Fable* (2002), *A Concise Encyclopedia* (2004) and *A Dictionary of Business and Management* (2006). He lives in Buckinghamshire with his wife and three children.

Other titles in the *Perfect* series

Perfect Answers to Interview Questions – Max Eggert
Perfect Babies' Names – Rosalind Fergusson
Perfect Best Man – George Davidson
Perfect CV – Max Eggert
Perfect Interview – Max Eggert
Perfect Numerical Test Results – Joanna Moutafi and Ian Newcombe
Perfect Personality Profiles – Helen Baron
Perfect Psychometric Test Results – Joanna Moutafi and Ian Newcombe
Perfect Pub Quiz – David Pickering
Perfect Punctuation – Stephen Curtis
Perfect Wedding Speeches and Toasts – George Davidson

Perfect
Readings for
Weddings

Jonathan Law

BOOKS

Published by Random House Books 2007

2 4 6 8 10 9 7 5 3 1

Copyright of items reprinted in the anthology rests with the
authors and other rights holders as stated in the acknowledgements
on pp. 201–03, which constitute an extension of this copyright page

Introduction and editorial material copyright
© Market House Books Ltd 2007

This book is sold subject to the condition that it shall not,
by way of trade or otherwise, be lent, resold, hired out,
or otherwise circulated without the publisher's prior
consent in any form of binding or cover other than that
in which it is published and without a similar condition,
including this condition, being imposed on the
subsequent purchaser

First published in the United Kingdom in 2007 by
Random House Books

Random House Books
Random House, 20 Vauxhall Bridge Road,
London SW1V 2SA

www.randomhouse.co.uk

Addresses for companies within The Random House Group Limited
can be found at: www.randomhouse.co.uk/offices.htm

The Random House Group Limited Reg. No. 954009

A CIP catalogue record for this book
is available from the British Library

ISBN 9781905211098

The Random House Group Limited makes every effort to ensure that the
papers used in its books are made from trees that have been legally sourced
from well-managed and credibly certified forests. Our paper procurement
policy can be found at: www.randomhouse.co.uk/paper.htm

Printed in the UK by CPI Bookmarque, Croydon, CR0 4TD

Contents

Introduction

Everybody wants their wedding day to be perfect and an important part of getting it right is finding the best readings for the occasion. Choosing words that are at once memorable, personal, and wholly appropriate to the occasion can seem a daunting task, especially when there are so many other arrangements to be made. To make the job easy, this book provides a collection of wise, witty, and inspirational readings suitable for weddings of every kind – church ceremonies, secular weddings, services of blessing, and same-sex civil ceremonies. The readings selected have been made as varied as possible, to suit the varied requirements of those using the book. Although the selection includes many Bible and other readings perfect for traditional church weddings, it also recognizes that many people will not be getting married for the first time; many will not be young; and many will be from non-Christian backgrounds.

The readings also vary enormously in terms of tone, style, and authorship; sources range from classic poetry to contemporary authors and there has been a determined effort to leaven the familiar and well loved with the fresh and unexpected. What all the readings have in common is a certain literary quality and – we hope – a certain toughness and integrity. While a wedding is nearly always an emotional occasion, it should not be a sentimental one, and silly verse of the greetings-card variety has therefore been eschewed.

In choosing readings for your wedding, you will inevitably want to find words that express your own beliefs about marriage and your personal feelings the commitment you are entering into. However, the choice of readings will also be governed by the type of wedding you are having – religious, civil, or non-traditional. To help you make the right choices, the legal and other constraints affecting each type of wedding are explained below; there is also a useful guide on p. 58 indicating which of the readings in this book are most appropriate for the various types of ceremony.

Church weddings

All church weddings must include at least one reading from the Bible. The usual custom – especially if communion is celebrated – is to have one reading from the Gospels and one from either the Old Testament or the New Testament epistles (sometimes both). To make choosing Bible readings as straightforward as possible, this book provides a generous selection of the most popular and appropriate passages in each category (Old Testament, Gospel, epistle). Each reading is given in both the Authorized (King James) Version and one of the standard modern translations.

At the discretion of the priest or minister, a suitable reading from a source other than the Bible may also be included. The reading need not be explicitly religious but must be compatible with the idea of Christian marriage and the dignity of the occasion. For these reasons, the minister's approval should be sought at an early stage and his or her decision must be regarded as final.

The use of non-Biblical readings has also become quite common in the services of blessing that many couples choose to go through after a civil marriage ceremony. Here the content of the service tends to be quite flexible – partly because the ceremony has no legal or sacramental significance, but also because traditions are less established. The same is true for the increasingly popular practice in which couples publicly renew their vows as part of a religious service (usually at a significant anniversary, but sometimes because the marriage has survived a troubled period). On such occasions, the reading of passages that have been chosen to reflect the couple's personal experience of married life can be particularly appropriate (and particularly moving).

Other religious traditions

The reading of prayers, blessings, and passages from the scriptures plays an important part in traditional Jewish, Muslim, Hindu, and Sikh weddings. In such ceremonies, the words to be used are prescribed by custom or authority and there is no tradition of using additional readings to personalize the occasion. Modern Jewish weddings in the Reform tradition provide a notable exception; in particular, many couples choose to adapt the traditional *ketubah* – the marriage contract read aloud before or during the ceremony – in a way that reflects their personal values and beliefs.

In Buddhism marriage is regarded as a social rather than a religious event. This means that there are many regional customs but no prescribed rituals for the occasion.

Civil weddings

By law, civil marriage ceremonies held in a UK registry office or other approved venue cannot include any material of a religious nature. This condition is applied very strictly and means that readings or vows containing even the vaguest references to a deity or an afterlife are not permitted (some registrars may be flexible where the language used is clearly figurative). Another constraint may be time – most registry office weddings allow for only one or two short readings. Any material that you wish to use should be submitted to the superintendent registrar well in advance and his or her decision is final.

Following a series of reforms to the law, civil weddings in all parts of the UK can now be held in certain licensed premises such as castles, hotels, and stately homes as well as in registry offices. Apart from providing a more atmospheric setting, this usually allows for a longer, more personalized ceremony and greater flexibility in the use of readings and music. However, it should be remembered that exactly the same rules about the use of religious material apply as in the registry office.

Same-sex civil ceremonies

Since December 2005 UK law has provided for the legal recognition of same-sex partnerships on terms that differ very little from civil marriage. The legal formalities are carried out in a registry office or other licensed premises and may be accompanied by readings, vows, and music. Religious content is not permitted and the registrar will usually advise couples to avoid the words 'marriage' and 'wedding'. Although there is no official procedure for doing so, some sympathetic clergy are willing to conduct a service of blessing for civil partners who wish to add a religious dimension.

This collection includes a number of readings chosen especially for their appropriateness to a same-sex ceremony (see, again, the guide on p. 58); otherwise, most of the passages identified here as being suitable for a civil marriage would be perfectly fitting.

Alternative ceremonies

For those who are clear that they do not want to be married in church but fear that a standard civil ceremony will be too restrictive, a number of options are available. New Age, pagan, and humanist wedding ceremonies all allow couples to express their commitment in the context of their personal beliefs. Examples of such ceremonies are widely available on the Internet and can be adapted in almost any way that the couple sees fit; there are also organizations and individuals who specialize in the planning of such events (again, the Internet is probably the first place to look). A few well chosen readings can play an extremely important part in such a ceremony and here there will be no restrictions on their content. This being the case, however, couples should take care that self-expression does not tip over into self-indulgence; you do not want to bore or alienate your guests. Be clear, too, that such alternative ceremonies have no legal status; for the marriage to be recognized in law, there must be a brief visit to the registry office, where the statutory declarations can be made.

Once you have chosen your readings, the next question will probably be who you should ask to read them. Here there are several considerations. Is there, for example, a close friend or family member who has not been given a specific role on the day? If so, this may be a very good way of involving them more closely. Also, consider whether any of your guests has a particular talent for speaking in public. Remember that not everyone will be comfortable with the idea of reading in front of a large audience, and that even experienced speakers may quail a little when presented with (for example) a piece of 17th-century poetry. As far as you can, therefore, try to match readers to readings, or vice versa. If you feel equally drawn to several readings, it can be a good policy to give each of your readers several alternatives and allow them to make the final choice.

Lastly, what advice should be given to the person who has been asked to read at a wedding or similar occasion? The best preparation is undoubtedly to make sure that you understand the passage in question – if you do, the correct emphasis and intonation should follow quite naturally. Try to obtain a copy of the passage well in advance and read it through several times – first to yourself and then out loud. Remember that when speaking in public it is always a good idea to speak slightly more slowly and more loudly than seems quite necessary; this will counteract any nervous tendency to gabble or mumble. Read with some expression, but don't attempt to give a dramatic performance. Speak to the people in front of you rather than to the back of the room, and try to move your eyes over your audience so that nobody feels left out. Because direct eye contact can seem confrontational, experienced speakers sometimes use the trick of speaking to the ears or shoulders of individual members of the audience. Above all, try to relax and enjoy the important contribution you are making to a really special occasion.

J.L.
2007

Bible Readings

Readings from the Old Testament
(including the Old Testament Apocrypha)

Male and Female

GENESIS 1. 26-28, 31a

(Authorized Version)

And God said, Let us make man in our image, after our likeness: and let them have dominion over the fish of the sea, and over the fowl of the air, and over the cattle, and over all the earth, and over every creeping thing that creepeth upon the earth.

So God created man in his own image, in the image of God created he him; male and female created he them.

And God blessed them, and God said unto them, Be fruitful, and multiply, and replenish the earth, and subdue it: and have dominion over the fish of the sea, and over the fowl of the air, and over every living thing that moveth upon the earth...

And God saw every thing that he had made, and, behold, it was very good.

(New Revised Standard Version)

Then God said, 'Let us make humankind in our image, according to our likeness: and let them have dominion over the fish of the sea, and over the birds of the air, and over the cattle, and over all the wild animals of the earth, and over every creeping thing that creeps upon the earth.'

So God created humankind in his image,
in the image of God he created them;
male and female he created them.

God blessed them, and God said to them, 'Be fruitful and multiply, and fill the earth and subdue it; and have dominion over the fish of the sea and over the birds of the air and over every living thing that moves upon the earth.'…God saw everything that he had made, and indeed, it was very good. And there was evening and there was morning, the sixth day.

One Flesh

GENESIS 2. 18-25

(Authorized Version)

And the LORD God said, It is not good that the man should be alone; I will make him an help meet for him.

And out of the ground the LORD God formed every beast of the field, and every fowl of the air, and brought them unto Adam to see what he would call them: and whatsoever Adam called every living creature, that was the name thereof.

And Adam gave names to all cattle, and to the fowl of the air, and to every beast of the field; but for Adam there was not found an help meet for him.

And the LORD God caused a deep sleep to fall upon Adam, and he slept: and he took one of his ribs, and closed up the flesh instead thereof;

And the rib, which the LORD God had taken from man, made he a woman, and brought her unto the man.

And Adam said, This is now bone of my bones, and flesh of my flesh: she shall be called Woman, because she was taken out of Man.

Therefore shall a man leave his father and his mother, and shall cleave unto his wife: and they shall be one flesh.

And they were both naked, the man and his wife, and were not ashamed.

(New Revised Standard Version)

Then the LORD God said, 'It is not good that the man should be alone; I will make him a helper as his partner.' So out of the ground the LORD God formed every animal of the field and every bird of the air, and brought them to the man to see what he would call them; and whatever the man called each living creature, that was its name. The man gave names to all cattle, and to the birds of the air, and to every animal of the field; but for the man there was not found a helper as his partner. So the LORD God caused a deep sleep to fall upon the man, and he slept; then he took one of his ribs and closed up its place with flesh. And the rib that the LORD God had taken from the man he made into a woman and brought her to the man. Then the man said,

> 'This at last is bone of my bones
> and flesh of my flesh;
> this one shall be called Woman,
> for out of Man this one was taken.'

Therefore a man leaves his father and his mother and clings to his wife, and they become one flesh. And the man and his wife were both naked, and were not ashamed.

An Everlasting Covenant

GENESIS 9. 8-17

(Authorized Version)

And God spake unto Noah, and to his sons with him, saying,

And I, behold, I establish my covenant with you, and with your seed after you;

And with every living creature that is with you, of the fowl, of the cattle, and of every beast of the earth with you; from all that go out of the ark, to every beast of the earth.

And I will establish my covenant with you; neither shall all flesh be cut off any more by the waters of a flood; neither shall there any more be a flood to destroy the earth.

And God said, This is the token of the covenant which I make between me and you and every living creature that is with you, for perpetual generations:

I do set my bow in the cloud, and it shall be for a token of a covenant between me and the earth.

And it shall come to pass, when I bring a cloud over the earth, that the bow shall be seen in the cloud:

And I will remember my covenant, which is between me and you and every living creature of all flesh; and the waters shall no more become a flood to destroy all flesh.

And the bow shall be in the cloud; and I will look upon it, that I may remember the everlasting covenant between God and every living creature of all flesh that is upon the earth.

And God said unto Noah, This is the token of the covenant, which I have established between me and all flesh that is upon the earth.

(New Revised Standard Version)

Then God said to Noah and to his sons with him, 'As for me, I am establishing my covenant with you and your descendants after you, and with every living creature that is with you, the birds, the domestic animals, and every animal of the earth with you, as many as came out of the ark. I establish my covenant with you, that never again shall all flesh be cut off by the waters of a flood, and never again shall there be a flood to destroy the earth.' God said, 'This is the sign of the covenant that I make between me and you and every living creature that is with you, for all future generations: I have set my bow in the clouds, and it shall be a sign of the covenant between me and the earth. When I bring clouds over the earth and the bow is seen in the clouds, I will remember my covenant that is between me and you and every living creature of all flesh; and the waters shall never again become a flood to destroy all flesh. When the bow is in the clouds, I will see it and remember the everlasting covenant between God and every living creature of all flesh that is on the earth.' God said to Noah, 'This is the sign of the covenant that I have established between me and all flesh that is on the earth.'

Where You Go, I Will Go

RUTH 1. 16-17

(Authorized Version)

And Ruth said, Entreat me not to leave thee, or to return from following after thee: for whither thou goest, I will go; and where thou
lodgest, I will lodge: thy people shall be my people, and thy God my
God:

Where thou diest, will I die, and there will I be buried: the LORD do so to me, and more also, if aught but death part thee and me.

(New Revised Standard Version)

But Ruth said,

'Do not press me to leave you
or to turn back from following you!
Where you go, I will go;
where you lodge, I will lodge;
your people shall be my people,
and your God my God.
Where you die, I will die –
there will I be buried.
May the LORD do thus and so to me,
and more as well,
if even death parts me from you!'

The Way of the Righteous

PSALMS 1. 1-6

(Authorized Version)

Blessed is the man that walketh not in the counsel of the ungodly, nor standeth in the way of sinners, nor sitteth in the seat of the scornful.

But his delight is in the law of the LORD; and in his law doth he meditate day and night.

And he shall be like a tree planted by the rivers of water that bringeth forth his fruit in his season; his leaf also shall not wither; and whatsoever he doeth shall prosper.

The ungodly are not so: but are like the chaff which the wind driveth
   away.
Therefore the ungodly shall not stand in the judgment, nor sinners in
   the congregation of the righteous.
For the LORD knoweth the way of the righteous: but the way of the
   ungodly shall perish.

(New Revised Standard Version)

Happy are those
   who do not follow the advice of the wicked,
or take the path that sinners tread,
   or sit in the seat of scoffers;
but their delight is in the law of the LORD,
   and on his law they meditate day and night.
They are like trees
   planted by streams of water,
which yield their fruit in its season,
   and their leaves do not wither.
In all that they do, they prosper.

The wicked are not so,
   but are like chaff that the wind drives away.
Therefore the wicked will not stand in the judgement,
   nor sinners in the congregation of the righteous;
for the LORD watches over the way of the righteous,
   but the way of the wicked will perish.

Let the People Praise Thee

PSALMS 67. 1-7

(Authorized Version).

God be merciful unto us, and bless us; and cause his face to shine upon
us;

That thy way may be known upon earth, thy saving health among all
nations.

Let the people praise thee, O God; let all the people praise thee.

O let the nations be glad and sing for joy: for thou shalt judge the
people righteously, and govern the nations upon earth.

Let the people praise thee, O God; let all the people praise thee.

Then shall the earth yield her increase; and God, even our own God,
shall bless us.

God shall bless us; and all the ends of the earth shall fear him.

(New Revised Standard Version).

May God be gracious to us and bless us
  and make his face to shine upon us,
that your way may be known upon earth,
  your saving power among all nations.
Let the peoples praise you, O God;
  let all the peoples praise you.

Let the nations be glad and sing for joy,
  for you judge the peoples with equity
  and guide the nations upon earth.
Let the peoples praise you, O God;
  let all the peoples praise you.

The earth has yielded its increase;
  God, our God, has blessed us.
May God continue to bless us;
  let all the ends of the earth revere him.

I Will Lift Up Mine Eyes

PSALMS 121. 1-8

(Authorized Version)

I will lift up mine eyes unto the hills, from whence cometh my help.
My help cometh from the LORD, which made heaven and earth.
He will not suffer thy foot to be moved: he that keepeth thee will not
    slumber.
Behold, he that keepeth Israel shall neither slumber nor sleep.
The LORD is thy keeper: the LORD is thy shade upon thy right hand.
The sun shall not smite thee by day, nor the moon by night.
The LORD shall preserve thee from all evil: he shall preserve thy soul.
The LORD shall preserve thy going out and thy coming in from this
    time forth, and even for evermore.

(New Revised Standard Version)

I lift up my eyes to the hills –
    from where will my help come?
My help comes from the LORD,
    who made heaven and earth.

He will not let your foot be moved;
    he who keeps you will not slumber.
He who keeps Israel
    will neither slumber nor sleep.

The LORD is your keeper;
    the LORD is your shade at your right hand.
The sun shall not strike you by day,
    nor the moon by night.

The LORD will keep you from all evil;
    he will keep your life.
The LORD will keep
    your going out and your coming in
    from this time on and for evermore.

As a Fruitful Vine

PSALMS 128. 1-6

(Authorized Version)

Blessed is every one that feareth the LORD; that walketh in his ways.
For thou shalt eat the labour of thine hands: happy shalt thou be, and
    it shall be well with thee.
Thy wife shall be as a fruitful vine by the sides of thine house: thy chil-
    dren like olive plants round about thy table.
Behold, that thus shall the man be blessed that feareth the LORD.
The LORD shall bless thee out of Zion: and thou shalt see the good of
    Jerusalem all the days of thy life.
Yea, thou shalt see thy children's children, and peace upon Israel.

(New Revised Standard Version)

Happy is everyone who fears the LORD,
    who walks in his ways.
You shall eat the fruit of the labour of your hands;
    you shall be happy, and it shall go well with you.

Your wife will be like a fruitful vine
    within your house;
Your children will be like olive shoots
    around your table.

Thus shall the man be blessed
who fears the LORD.

The LORD bless you from Zion.
May you see the prosperity of Jerusalem
all the days of your life.
May you see your children's children.
Peace be upon Israel!

His Steadfast Love Endures For Ever

PSALMS 136. 1-9, 26

(Authorized Version).

O give thanks unto the LORD; for he is good; for his mercy endureth for ever.

O give thanks unto the God of gods: for his mercy endureth for ever.

O give thanks to the Lord of lords: for his mercy endureth for ever.

To him who alone doeth great wonders: for his mercy endureth for ever.

To him that by wisdom made the heavens: for his mercy endureth for ever.

To him that stretched out the earth above the waters: for his mercy endureth for ever.

To him that made great lights: for his mercy endureth for ever.

The sun to rule by day: for his mercy endureth for ever.

The moon and stars to rule by night: for his mercy endureth for ever…

O give thanks unto the God of heaven: for his mercy endureth for ever.

(New Revised Standard Version)

O give thanks to the LORD, for he is good,
    for his steadfast love endures for ever.
O give thanks to the God of gods,
    for his steadfast love endures for ever.
O give thanks to the Lord of lords,
    for his steadfast love endures for ever;
who alone does great wonders,
    for his steadfast love endures for ever;
who by understanding made the heavens,
    for his steadfast love endures for ever;
who spread out the earth on the waters,
    for his steadfast love endures for ever;
who made great lights,
    for his steadfast love endures for ever;
the sun to rule over the day,
    for his steadfast love endures for ever;
the moon and stars to rule over the night,
    for his steadfast love endures for ever…
O give thanks to the God of heaven
    for his steadfast love endures for ever.

Praise Ye the Lord

PSALMS 150. 1-6

(Authorized Version)

Praise ye the LORD. Praise God in his sanctuary: praise him in the firmament of his power.
Praise him for his mighty acts: praise him according to his excellent greatness.

Praise him with the sound of the trumpet: praise him with the psaltery and harp.

Praise him with the timbrel and dance: praise him with stringed instruments and organs.

Praise him upon the loud cymbals: praise him upon the high sounding cymbals.

Let every thing that hath breath praise the LORD. Praise ye the LORD.

(New Revised Standard Version)

Praise the LORD!
Praise God in his sanctuary;
    praise him in his mighty firmament!
Praise him for his mighty deeds;
    praise him according to his surpassing greatness!

Praise him with trumpet sound;
    praise him with lute and harp!
Praise him with tambourine and dance;
    praise him with strings and pipe!
Praise him with clanging cymbals;
    praise him with loud clashing cymbals!
Let everything that breathes praise the LORD!
Praise the LORD!

Rejoice with the Wife of thy Youth

PROVERBS 5. 18-19

(Authorized Version)

Let thy fountain be blessed: and rejoice with the wife of thy youth.
Let her be as the loving hind and pleasant roe; let her breasts satisfy thee at all times; and be thou ravished always with her love.

(New Revised Standard Version)

Let your fountain be blessed,
    and rejoice in the wife of your youth,
    a lovely deer, a graceful doe.
May her breasts satisfy you at all times;
    may you be intoxicated always by her love.

A Virtuous Woman

PROVERBS 31. 10-31

(Authorized Version)

Who can find a virtuous woman? for her price is far above rubies.

The heart of her husband doth safely trust in her, so that he shall have no need of spoil.

She will do him good and not evil all the days of her life.

She seeketh wool, and flax, and worketh willingly with her hands.

She is like the merchants' ships; she bringeth her food from afar.

She riseth also while it is yet night, and giveth meat to her household, and a portion to her maidens.

She considereth a field, and buyeth it: with the fruit of her hands she planteth a vineyard.

She girdeth her loins with strength, and strengtheneth her arms.

She perceiveth that her merchandise is good: her candle goeth not out by night.

She layeth her hands to the spindle, and her hands hold the distaff.

She stretcheth out her hand to the poor; yea, she reacheth forth her hands to the needy.

She is not afraid of the snow for her household: for all her household are clothed with scarlet.

She maketh herself coverings of tapestry; her clothing is silk and purple.

Her husband is known in the gates, when he sitteth among the elders of the land.

She maketh fine linen, and selleth it; and delivereth girdles unto the merchant.

Strength and honour are her clothing; and she shall rejoice in time to come.

She openeth her mouth with wisdom; and in her tongue is the law of kindness.

She looketh well to the ways of her household, and eateth not the bread of idleness.

Her children arise up, and call her blessed; her husband also, and he praiseth her.

Many daughters have done virtuously, but thou excellest them all.

Favour is deceitful, and beauty is vain: but a woman that feareth the LORD, she shall be praised.

Give her of the fruit of her hands; and let her own works praise her in the gates.

(New Revised Standard Version).

A capable wife who can find?
    She is far more precious than jewels.
The heart of her husband trusts in her,
    and he will have no lack of gain.
She does him good, and not harm,
    all the days of her life.
She seeks wool and flax,
    and works with willing hands.
She is like the ships of the merchant,
    she brings her food from far away.
She rises while it is still night
    and provides food for her household
    and tasks for her servant-girls.

She considers a field and buys it;
    with the fruit of her hands she plants a vineyard.
She girds herself with strength,
    and makes her arms strong.
She perceives that her merchandise is profitable.
    Her lamp does not go out at night.
She puts her hands to the distaff,
    and her hands hold the spindle.
She opens her hand to the poor,
    and reaches out her hands to the needy.
She is not afraid for her household when it snows,
    for all her household are clothed in crimson.
She makes herself coverings; her clothing is fine linen and purple.
Her husband is known in the city gates,
    taking his seat among the elders of the land.
She makes linen garments and sells them;
    she supplies the merchant with sashes.
Strength and dignity are her clothing,
    and she laughs at the time to come.
She opens her mouth with wisdom,
    and the teaching of kindness is on her tongue.
She looks well to the ways of her household,
    and does not eat the bread of idleness.
Her children rise up and call her happy;
    her husband too, and he praises her;
'Many women have done excellently,
    but you surpass them all.'
Charm is deceitful, and beauty is vain,
    but a woman who fears the LORD is to be praised.
Give her a share in the fruit of her hands,
    and let her works praise her in the city gates.

To Every Thing there Is a Season

ECCLESIASTES 3. 1-8

(Authorized Version)

To every thing there is a season, and a time to every purpose under the heaven.

A time to be born, and a time to die; a time to plant, and a time to pluck up that which is planted;

A time to kill, and a time to heal; a time to break down, and a time to build up;

A time to weep, and a time to laugh; a time to mourn, and a time to dance;

A time to cast away stones, and a time to gather stones together; a time to embrace, and a time to refrain from embracing.

A time to get, and a time to lose; a time to keep, and a time to cast away;

A time to rend, and a time to sew; a time to keep silence, and a time to speak;

A time to love, and a time to hate; a time of war, and a time of peace.

(New Revised Standard Version)

For everything there is a season, and a time to every matter under heaven:

a time to be born, and a time to die;

a time to plant, and a time to pluck up what is planted;

a time to kill, and a time to heal;

a time to break down, and a time to build up;

a time to weep, and a time to laugh;

a time to mourn, and a time to dance;

a time to throw away stones, and a time to gather stones together;

a time to embrace, and a time to refrain from embracing.

a time to seek, and a time to lose;
a time to keep, and a time to throw away;
a time to tear, and a time to sew;
a time to keep silence, and a time to speak;
a time to love, and a time to hate;
a time for war, and a time for peace.

Two Are Better than One

ECCLESIASTES 4. 9-12

(Authorized Version)

Two are better than one; because they have a good reward for their labour.
For if they fall, the one will lift up his fellow: but woe to him that is alone when he falleth; for he hath not another to help him up.
Again, if two lie together, then they have heat: but how can one be warm alone?
And if one prevail against him, two shall withstand him; and a three-fold cord is not quickly broken.

(New Revised Standard Version)

Two are better than one, because they have a good reward for their toil. For if they fall, one will lift up the other; but woe to one who is alone and falls and does not have another to help. Again, if two lie together, they keep warm; but how can one keep warm alone? And though one might prevail against another, two will withstand one. A threefold cord is not quickly broken.

Arise, My Love

SONG OF SOLOMON 2. 10-14, 16-17

(Authorized Version)

My beloved spake, and said unto me, Rise up, my love, my fair one, and come away.

For, lo, the winter is past, the rain is over and gone;

The flowers appear on the earth; the time of the singing of birds is come, and the voice of the turtle is heard in our land;

The fig tree putteth forth her green figs, and the vines with the tender grape give a good smell. Arise, my love, my fair one, and come away.

O my dove that art in the clefts of the rock, in the secret places of the stairs, let me see thy countenance, let me hear thy voice; for sweet is thy voice, and thy countenance is comely…

My beloved is mine, and I am his: he feedeth among the lilies.

Until the day break, and the shadows flee away, turn my beloved, and be thou like a roe or a young hart upon the mountains of Bether.

(New Revised Standard Version)

My beloved speaks and says to me:
'Arise, my love, my fair one,
    and come away;
for now the winter is past,
    the rain is over and gone.
The flowers appear on the earth;
    the time of singing has come,
and the voice of the turtle-dove
    is heard in our land.
The fig tree puts forth its figs,
    and the vines are in blossom;
    they give forth fragrance.

Arise, my love, my fair one,
 and come away.
O my dove, in the clefts of the rock,
 in the covert of the cliff,
let me see your face,
 let me hear your voice;
for your voice is sweet,
 and your face is lovely…
My beloved is mine and I am his;
 he pastures his flock among the lilies.
Until the day breathes
 and the shadows flees,
turn, my beloved, be like a gazelle
 or a young stag on the cleft mountains.

Many Waters Cannot Quench Love

SONG OF SOLOMON 8. 6-7

(Authorized Version)

Set me as a seal upon thine heart, as a seal upon thine arm: for love is
 strong as death; jealousy is cruel as the grave: the coals thereof are
 coals of fire, which hath a most vehement flame.
Many waters cannot quench love, neither can the floods drown it: if a
 man would give all the substance of his house for love, it would
 utterly be contemned.

(New Revised Standard Version)

Set me as a seal upon your heart,
 as a seal upon your arm;

for love is strong as death,
    passion fierce as the grave.
Its flashes are flashes of fire,
    a raging flame.
Many waters cannot quench love,
    neither can floods drown it.
If one offered for love
    all the wealth of one's house,
    it would be utterly scorned.

I Will Greatly Rejoice

ISAIAH 61. 10-11

(Authorized Version)

I will greatly rejoice in the LORD, my soul shall be joyful in my God; for
he hath clothed me with the garments of salvation, he hath covered
me with the robe of righteousness, as a bridegroom decketh himself
with ornaments, and as a bride adorneth herself with her jewels.
For as the earth bringeth forth her bud, and as the garden causeth the
things that are sown in it to spring forth; so the Lord GOD will cause
righteousness and praise to spring forth before all the nations.

(New Revised Standard Version)

I will greatly rejoice in the LORD,
    my whole being shall exult in my God;
for he has clothed me with the garments of salvation,
    he has covered me with the robe of righteousness,
as a bridegroom decks himself with a garland,
    and as a bride adorns herself with her jewels.

For as the earth brings forth its shoots,
  and as a garden causes what is sown in it to spring up,
so the Lord GOD will cause righteousness and praise
  to spring up before all the nations.

As the Bridegroom Rejoices over the Bride

ISAIAH 62. 1-5

(Authorized Version)

For Zion's sake will I will not hold my peace, and for Jerusalem's sake I will not rest until the righteousness thereof go forth as brightness, and the salvation thereof as a lamp that burneth.

And the Gentiles shall see thy righteousness, and all kings thy glory: and thou shalt be called by a new name, which the mouth of the LORD shall name.

Thou shalt also be a crown of glory in the hand of the LORD, and a royal diadem in the hand of thy God.

Thou shalt no more be termed Forsaken; neither shall thy land any more be termed Desolate: but thou shalt be called Hephzibah, and thy land called Beulah: for the LORD delighteth in thee, and thy land shall be married.

For as a young man marrieth a virgin, so shall thy sons marry thee: and as the bridegroom rejoiceth over the bride, so shall thy God rejoice over thee.

(New Revised Standard Version)

For Zion's sake I will not keep silent,
and for Jerusalem's sake I will not rest,
until her vindication shines out like the dawn,
and her salvation like a burning torch.
The nations shall see your vindication,
and all the Kings your glory;
and you shall be called by a new name
that the mouth of the LORD will give.
You shall be a crown of beauty in the hand of the LORD,
and a royal diadem in the hand of your God.
You shall no more be termed Forsaken,
and your land shall no more be termed Desolate;
but you shall be called My Delight Is in Her,
and your land Married;
for the LORD delights in you,
and your land shall be married.
For as a young man marries a young woman,
so shall your builder marry you,
and as the bridegroom rejoices over the bride,
so shall your God rejoice over you.

A New Covenant

JEREMIAH 31. 31-34

(Authorized Version)

Behold, the days come, saith the LORD, that I will make a new covenant
with the house of Israel, and with the house of Judah:
Not according to the covenant that I made with their fathers in the day

that I took them by the hand to bring them out of the land of Egypt; which my covenant they brake, although I was an husband unto them, saith the LORD:

But this shall be the covenant that I will make with the house of Israel; After those days, saith the LORD, I will put my law in their inward parts, and write it in their hearts; and will be their God, and they shall be my people.

And they shall teach no more every man his neighbour, and every man his brother, saying, Know the LORD: for they shall all know me, from the least of them unto the greatest of them, saith the LORD: for I will forgive their iniquity, and I will remember their sin no more.

(New Revised Standard Version)

The days are surely coming says the LORD, when I will make a new covenant with the house of Israel and the house of Judah. It will not be like the covenant that I made with their ancestors, when I took them by the hand to bring them out of the land of Egypt – a covenant that they broke, though I was their husband, says the LORD. But this is the covenant that I will make with the house of Israel after those days, says the LORD: I will put my law within them, and I will write it on their hearts; and I will be their God, and they shall be my people. No longer shall they teach one another, or say to each other 'Know the LORD', for they shall all know me, from the least of them to the greatest, says the LORD; for I will forgive their iniquity, and remember their sin no more.

I Will Take You for My Wife for Ever

HOSEA 2. 18-20

(Authorized Version)

And in that day will I make a covenant for them with the beasts of the field, and with the fowls of heaven, and with the creeping things of the ground: and I will break the bow and the sword and the battle out of the earth, and will make them to lie down safely.

And I will betroth thee unto me for ever; yea, I will betroth thee unto me in righteousness, and in judgment, and in lovingkindness, and in mercies.

I will even betroth thee unto me in faithfulness: and thou shalt know the LORD.

(New Revised Standard Version)

I will make for you a covenant on that day with the wild animals, the birds of the air, and the creeping things of the ground; and I will abolish the bow, the sword, and war from the land; and I will make you lie down in safety. And I will take you for my wife for ever; I will take you for my wife in righteousness and in justice, in steadfast love, and in mercy. I will take you for my wife in faithfulness; and you shall know the LORD.

The Prayer of Tobias and Sara

TOBIT 8. 4-8

(Authorized Version)

And after that they were both shut in together, Tobias rose out of the bed, and said, Sister, arise, and let us pray that God would have pity on us.

Then began Tobias to say, Blessed art thou, O God of our fathers, and blessed is thy holy and glorious name for ever; let the heavens bless thee, and all thy creatures.

Thou madest Adam, and gavest him Eve his wife for an helper and stay: of them came mankind: thou hast said, It is not good that man should be alone; let us make unto him an aid like unto himself.

And now, O Lord, I take not this my sister for lust but uprightly: therefore mercifully ordain that we may become aged together.

And she said with him, Amen.

(New Revised Standard Version)

When the parents had gone out and shut the door of the room, Tobias got out of bed and said to Sarah, 'Sister, get up, and let us pray and implore our Lord that he grant us mercy and safety.' So she got up, and they began to pray and implore that they might be kept safe. Tobias began by saying,

'Blessed are you, O God of our ancestors,
    and blessed is your name in all generations forever.
Let the heavens and the whole creation bless you forever.
You made Adam, and for him you made his wife Eve as a
    helper and support.
From the two of them the human race has sprung.
You said, "It is not good that the man should be alone;
    let us make a helper for him like himself."

I now am taking this kinswoman of mine,
    not because of lust,
    but with sincerity.
Grant that she and I may find mercy
    and that we may grow old together.'
And they both said, 'Amen, Amen.'

A Good Wife

ECCLESIASTICUS 26. 1-4, 13-18

(Authorized Version)

Blessed is the man that hath a virtuous wife, for the number of his days shall be double.

A virtuous woman rejoiceth her husband, and he shall fulfil the years of his life in peace.

A good wife is a good portion, which shall be given in the portion of them that fear the Lord.

Whether a man be rich or poor, if he have a good heart toward the Lord, he shall at all times rejoice with a cheerful countenance...

The grace of a wife delighteth her husband, and her discretion will fatten his bones.

A silent and loving woman is a gift of the Lord; and there is nothing so much worth as a mind well instructed.

A shamefaced and faithful woman is a double grace, and her continent mind cannot be valued.

As the sun when it ariseth in the high heaven; so is the beauty of a good wife in the ordering of her house.

As the clear light is upon the holy candlestick; so is the beauty of the face in ripe age.

As the golden pillars are upon the sockets of silver; so are the fair feet with a constant heart.

(New Revised Standard Version)

Happy is the husband of a good wife;
    the number of his days will be doubled.
A loyal wife brings joy to her husband,
    and he will complete his years in peace.
A good wife is a great blessing;
    she will be granted among the blessings of the man who
        fears the Lord.
Whether rich or poor, his heart is content,
    and at all times his face is cheerful…
A wife's charm delights her husband,
    and her skill puts flesh on his bones.
A silent wife is a gift from the Lord,
    and nothing is so precious as her self-discipline.
A modest wife adds charm to charm,
    and no scales can weigh the value of her chastity.
Like the sun rising in the heights of the LORD,
    so is the beautiful face on a stately figure.
Like golden pillars on silver bases,
    so are shapely legs and steadfast feet.

Readings from the Gospels

Blessed Are the Pure in Heart

MATTHEW 5. 1-12

(Authorized Version)

And seeing the multitude he went up into a mountain: and when he was set, his disciples came unto him:

And he opened his mouth and taught them, saying,

Blessed are the poor in spirit: for theirs is the kingdom of heaven.

Blessed are they that mourn: for they shall be comforted.

Blessed are the meek: for they shall inherit the earth.

Blessed are they which do hunger and thirst after righteousness: for they shall be filled.

Blessed are the merciful: for they shall obtain mercy.

Blessed are the pure in heart: for they shall see God.

Blessed are the peacemakers: for they shall be called the children of God.

Blessed are they which are persecuted for righteousness' sake: for theirs is the kingdom of heaven.

Blessed are ye, when men shall revile you, and persecute you, and shall say all manner of evil against you falsely, for my sake.

Rejoice, and be exceeding glad: for great is your reward in heaven: for so persecuted they the prophets which were before you.

(New Revised Standard Version)

When Jesus saw the crowds, he went up the mountain; and after he sat down, his disciples came to him. Then he began to speak, and taught them, saying:

'Blessed are the poor in spirit, for theirs is the kingdom of heaven.

'Blessed are those who mourn, for they will be comforted.

'Blessed are the meek, for they will inherit the earth.

'Blessed are those who hunger and thirst for righteousness, for they will be filled.

'Blessed are the merciful, for they will receive mercy.

'Blessed are the pure in heart, for they will see God.

'Blessed are the peacemakers, for they will be called children of God.

'Blessed are those who are persecuted for righteousness' sake, for theirs is the kingdom of heaven.

'Blessed are you when people revile you and persecute you and utter all kinds of evil against you falsely on my account. Rejoice and be glad, for your reward is great in heaven, for in the same way they persecuted the prophets who were before you.'

The Light of the World

MATTHEW 5. 13-16

(Authorized Version)

Ye are the salt of the earth: but if the salt have lost his savour, wherewith shall it be salted? it is thenceforth good for nothing, but to be cast out, and to be trodden under foot of men.

Ye are the light of the world. A city that is set on an hill cannot be hid.

Neither do men light a candle, and put it under a bushel, but on a candlestick; and it giveth light unto all that are in the house.

Let your light so shine before men, that they may see your good works, and glorify your Father which is in heaven.

(New Revised Standard Version)

'You are the salt of the earth; but if salt has lost its taste, how can its saltiness be restored? It is no longer good for anything, but is thrown out and trampled under foot.

'You are the light of the world. A city built on a hill cannot be hidden. No one after lighting a lamp puts it under the bushel basket, but on the lampstand and it gives light to all in the house. In the same way, let your light shine before others, so that they may see your good works and give glory to your Father in heaven.'

Treasures in Heaven

MATTHEW 6. 19-21, 24-25

(Authorized Version)

Lay not up for yourselves treasures upon earth, where moth and rust doth corrupt, and where thieves break through and steal:

But lay up for yourselves treasures in heaven, where neither moth nor rust doth corrupt, and where thieves do not break through nor steal:

For where your treasure is, there will your heart be also . . .

No man can serve two masters: for either he will hate the one, and love the other; or else he will hold to the one, and despise the other. Ye cannot serve God and mammon.

Therefore I say unto you, Take no thought for your life, what ye shall eat, or what ye shall drink; nor yet for your body, what ye shall put on. Is not the life more than meat, and the body than raiment?

Behold the fowls of the air: for they sow not, neither do they reap, nor gather into barns; yet your heavenly Father feedeth them. Are ye not much better than they?

Kansas City, KS Public
Library
913-295-8250

Library name: WESTWY
User ID: 33131006753325

Current time: 10/08/2019,
11:00
Date due: 10/29/2019,23:
59
Item ID: 23131117624425
Title: Poems and readings
for weddings and civil
partner

Current time: 10/08/2019,
11:00
Date due: 10/29/2019,23:
59
Item ID: 23131115594596
Title: Perfect readings for
weddings

Which of you by taking thought can add one cubit unto his stature?
And why take ye thought for raiment? Consider the lilies of the field,
   how they grow; they toil not, neither do they spin:
And yet I say unto you, That even Solomon in all his glory was not
   arrayed like one of these.

(New Revised Standard Version)

'Do not store up for yourselves treasures on earth, where moth and
rust consume and where thieves break in and steal; but store up for
yourselves treasures in heaven, where neither moth nor rust consumes
and where thieves do not break in and steal. For where your treasure is,
there your heart will be also . . .

   'No one can serve two masters; for a slave will either hate the one
and love the other, or be devoted to the one and despise the other. You
cannot serve God and wealth.

   'Therefore I tell you, do not worry about your life, what you will eat
or what you will drink, or about your body, what you will wear. Is not
life more than food, and the body more than clothing? Look at the
birds of the air; they neither sow nor reap nor gather into barns, and
yet your heavenly Father feeds them. Are you not of more value than
they? And can any of you by worrying add a single hour to your span
of life? And why do you worry about clothing? Consider the lilies of
the field, how they grow; they neither toil nor spin, yet I tell you, even
Solomon in all his glory was not clothed like one of these.'

A House Built upon a Rock

MATTHEW 7. 21, 24-27

(Authorized Version)

Not every one that saith unto me, Lord, Lord, shall enter into the kingdom of heaven; but he that doeth the will of my Father which is in heaven . . .

Therefore whosoever heareth these sayings of mine, and doeth them, I will liken him unto a wise man, which built his house upon a rock:

And the rain descended, and the floods came, and the winds blew, and beat upon that house; and it fell not: for it was founded upon a rock.

And every one that heareth these sayings of mine, and doeth them not, shall be likened unto a foolish man, which built his house upon the sand:

And the rain descended, and the floods came, and the winds blew, and beat upon that house; and it fell: and great was the fall of it.

(New Revised Standard Version)

'Not everyone who says to me "Lord, Lord" will enter the kingdom of heaven, but only one who does the will of my Father in heaven . . .

'Everyone then who hears these words of mine and acts on them will be like a wise man who built his house on rock.

'The rain fell, the floods came, and the winds blew and beat on that house, but it did not fall, because it had been founded on rock. And everyone who hears these words of mine and does not act on them will be like a foolish man who built his house on sand. The rain fell, and the floods came, and the winds blew and beat against that house, and it fell – and great was its fall!'

Two Commandments

MATTHEW 22. 34-40

(Authorized Version)

But when the Pharisees had heard that he had put the Sadducees to
silence, they were gathered together.

Then one of them, which was a lawyer, asked him a question, tempting
him, and saying,

Master, which is the great commandment in the law?

Jesus said unto him, Thou shalt love the Lord thy God with all thy
heart, and with all thy mind.

This is the first and great commandment.

And the second is like unto it, Thou shalt love thy neighbour as thyself.

On these two commandments hang all the law and the prophets.'

(New Revised Standard Version)

When the Pharisees heard that he had silenced the Sadducees, they
gathered together, and one of them, a lawyer, asked him a question to
test him. 'Teacher, which commandment in the law is the greatest?' He
said to him, '"You shall love the Lord your God with all your heart, and
with all your soul, and with all your mind." This is the greatest and first
commandment. And a second is like it: "You shall love your neighbour
as yourself." On these two commandments hang all the law and the
prophets.'

What God Hath Joined Together

MARK 10. 2-9

(Authorized Version)

And the Pharisees came to him, and asked him, Is it lawful for a man
to put away his wife? tempting him.

And he answered and said unto them, What did Moses command you?

And they said, Moses suffered to write a bill of divorcement, and to
put her away.

And Jesus answered and said unto them, For the hardness of your
heart he wrote you this precept.

But from the beginning of the creation God made them male and
female.

For this cause shall a man leave his father and mother, and cleave to his
wife;

And they twain shall be one flesh: so then they are no more twain, but
one flesh.

What therefore God hath joined together, let no man put asunder.

(New Revised Standard Version)

Some Pharisees came, and to test him they asked, 'Is it lawful for a man
to divorce his wife?' He answered them, 'What did Moses command
you?' They said 'Moses allowed a man to write a certificate of dismissal
and to divorce her.' But Jesus said to them, 'Because of your hardness
of heart he wrote this commandment for you. But from the beginning
of creation, "God made them male and female." "For this reason a man
shall leave his father and mother and be joined to his wife, and the two
shall become one flesh." So they are no longer two, but one flesh.
Therefore what God has joined together, let no one separate.'

The Marriage of Cana

JOHN 2. 1-11

(Authorized Version)

And the third day there was a marriage in Cana of Galilee; and the mother of Jesus was there:

And both Jesus was called, and his disciples, to the marriage.

And when they wanted wine, the mother of Jesus saith unto him, They have no wine.

Jesus saith unto her, Woman, what have I to do with thee? mine hour is not yet come.

His mother saith unto the servants, Whatsoever he saith unto you, do it.

And there were set there six waterpots of stone, after the manner of the purifying of the Jews, containing two or three firkins apiece.

Jesus saith unto them, Fill the waterpots with water. And they filled them up to the brim.

And he saith unto them, Draw out now, and bear unto the governor of the feast. And they bare it.

When the ruler of the feast had tasted the water that was made wine, and knew not whence it was: (but the servants which drew the water knew;) the governor of the feast called the bridegroom,

And saith unto him, Every man at the beginning doth set forth good wine; and when men have well drunk, then that which is worse: but thou hast kept the good wine until now.

This beginning of miracles did Jesus in Cana of Galilee, and manifested forth his glory; and his disciples believed on him.

(New Revised Standard Version)

On the third day there was a wedding in Cana of Galilee, and the mother of Jesus was there. Jesus and his disciples had also been invited to the wedding. When the wine gave out, the mother of Jesus said to him, 'They have no wine.' And Jesus said to her, 'Woman, what concern is that to you and to me? My hour has not yet come.' His mother said to the servants, 'Do whatever he tells you.' Now standing there were six stone water-jars for the Jewish rites of purification each holding twenty or thirty gallons. Jesus said to them, 'Fill the jars with water.' And they filled them up to the brim. He said to them, 'Now draw some out, and take it to the chief steward.' So they took it. When the steward tasted the water that had become wine, and did not know where it came from (though the servants who had drawn the water knew), the steward called the bridegroom and said to him, 'Everyone serves the good wine first, and then the inferior wine after the guests have become drunk. But you have kept the good wine until now.' Jesus did this, the first of his signs, in Cana of Galilee, and revealed his glory; and his disciples believed in him.

Greater Love Hath No Man

JOHN 15. 9-17

(Authorized Version)

As the Father hath loved me, so have I loved you: continue ye in my
   love.
If ye keep my commandments, ye shall abide in my love; even as I have
   kept my Father's commandments, and abide in his love.
These things have I spoken unto you, that my joy might remain in you,
   and that your joy might be full.

This is my commandment, That ye love one another, as I have loved you.

Greater love hath no man than this, that a man lay down his life for his friends.

Ye are my friends, if ye do whatsoever I command you.

Henceforth I call you not servants; for the servant knoweth not what his lord doeth, but I have called you friends, for all things that I have heard of my Father I have made known unto you.

Ye have not chosen me, but I have chosen you, and ordained you, that ye should go and bring forth fruit, and that your fruit should remain: that whatsoever ye shall ask of the Father in my name, he may give it you.

These things I command you, that ye love one another.

New Revised Standard Version)

'As the Father has loved me, so I have loved you; abide in my love. If you keep my commandments, you will abide in my love, just as I have kept my Father's commandments and abide in his love. I have said these things to you so that my joy may be in you, and that your joy may be complete.

'This is my commandment, that you love one another as I have loved you. No one has greater love that this, to lay down one's life for one's friends. You are my friends if you do what I command you. I do not call you servants any longer, because the servant does not know what the master is doing; but I have called you friends, because I have made known to you everything that I have heard from my Father. You did not choose me but I chose you. And I appointed you to go and bear fruit, fruit that will last, so that the Father will give you whatever you ask him in my name. I am giving you these commands so that you may love one another.'

Readings from the New Testament Epistles and Revelation

The Love of Christ

ROMANS 8. 35-39

(Authorized Version)

Who shall separate us from the love of Christ? shall tribulation, or distress, or persecution, or famine, or nakedness, or peril, or sword?
As it is written, For thy sake we are killed all the day long; we are accounted as sheep for the slaughter.
Nay, in all these things we are more than conquerors through him that loved us.
For I am persuaded, that neither death, nor life, nor angels, nor principalities, nor powers, nor things present, nor things to come,
Nor height, nor depth, nor any other creature, shall be able to separate us from the love of God, which is in Christ Jesus our Lord.

(New Revised Standard Version)

Who will separate us from the love of Christ? Will hardship, or distress, or persecution, or famine, or nakedness, or peril, or sword? As it is written,

'For your sake we are being killed all day long;
We are accounted as sheep to be slaughtered.'

No, in all these things we are more than conquerors through him who loved us. For I am convinced that neither death, nor life, nor angels, nor rulers, nor things present, nor things to come, nor powers, nor height, nor depth, nor anything else in all creation, will be able to separate us from the love of God in Christ Jesus our Lord.

Brotherly Love

ROMANS 12. 1-2, 9-21

(Authorized Version)

I beseech you therefore, brethren, by the mercies of God, that ye present your bodies a living sacrifice, holy, acceptable unto God, which is your reasonable service.

And be not conformed to this world: but be ye transformed by the renewing of your mind, that ye may prove what is that good, and acceptable, and perfect, will of God . . .

Let love be without dissimulation. Abhor that which is evil; cleave to that which is good.

Be kindly affectioned one to another with brotherly love; in honour preferring one another;

Not slothful in business; fervent in spirit; serving the Lord;

Rejoicing in hope; patient in tribulation; continuing instant in prayer;

Distributing to the necessity of saints; given to hospitality.

Bless them which persecute you: bless, and curse not.

Rejoice with them that do rejoice, and weep with them that weep.

Be of the same mind one toward another. Mind not high things, but condescend to men of low estate. Be not wise in your own conceits.

Recompense to no man evil for evil. Provide things honest in the sight of all men.

If it is possible, as much as lieth in you, live peaceably with all men.

Dearly beloved, avenge not yourselves, but rather give place unto wrath: for it is written, Vengeance is mine; I will repay, saith the Lord.

Therefore if thine enemy hunger, feed him; if he thirst give him drink: for in so doing thou shalt heap coals of fire on his head.

Be not overcome of evil, but overcome evil with good.

(New Revised Standard Version)

I appeal to you therefore, brothers and sisters, by the mercies of God, to present your bodies as a living sacrifice, holy and acceptable to God, which is your spiritual worship. Do not be conformed to this world, but be transformed by the renewing of your minds, so that you may discern what is the will of God – what is good and acceptable and perfect . . .

Let love be genuine; hate what is evil, hold fast to what is good; love one another with mutual affection; outdo one another in showing honour. Do not lag in zeal, be ardent in spirit, serve the Lord. Rejoice in hope, be patient in suffering, persevere in prayer. Contribute to the needs of the saints; extend hospitality to strangers.

Bless those who persecute you; bless and do not curse them. Rejoice with those who rejoice, weep with those who weep. Live in harmony with one another; do not be haughty, but associate with the lowly, do not claim to be wiser than you are. Do not repay anyone evil for evil, but take thought for what is noble in the sight of all. If it is possible, so far as it depends on you, live peaceably with all. Beloved, never avenge yourselves, but leave room for the wrath of God, for it is written, 'Vengeance is mine, I will repay, says the Lord.' No, if your enemies are hungry, feed them; if they are thirsty, give them something to drink; for by doing this you will heap burning coals on their heads.' Do not be overcome by evil, but overcome evil with good.

The Greatest of These

I CORINTHIANS 13. 1-13

(Authorized Version)

Though I speak with the tongues of men and of angels, and have not charity, I am become as sounding brass, or a tinkling cymbal.

And though I have the gift of prophecy, and understand all mysteries, and all knowledge; and though I have all faith, so that I could remove mountains, and have not charity, I am nothing.

And though I bestow all my goods to feed the poor, and though I give my body to be burned, and have not charity, it profiteth me nothing.

Charity suffereth long, and is kind; charity envieth not; charity vaunteth not itself, is not puffed up,

Doth not behave itself unseemly, seeketh not her own, is not easily provoked, thinketh no evil;

Rejoiceth not in iniquity, but rejoiceth in the truth;

Beareth all things, believeth all things, hopeth all things, endureth all things.

Charity never faileth; but whether there be prophecies, they shall fail; whether there be tongues, they shall cease; whether there be knowledge, it shall vanish away.

For we know in part, and we prophesy, in part.

But when that which is perfect is come, then that which is in part shall be done away.

When I was a child, I spake as a child, I understood as a child, I thought as a child: but when I became a man, I put away childish things.

For now we see through a glass, darkly; but then face to face: now I know in part; but then shall I know even as also I am known.

And now abideth faith, hope, charity, these three; but the greatest of these is charity.

This famous passage is often read in the Authorized Version but with 'love' substituted for 'charity' throughout.

(New Revised Standard Version)

If I speak in the tongues of mortals and of angels, but do not have love, I am a noisy gong or a clanging cymbal. And if I have prophetic powers, and understand all mysteries and all knowledge, and if I have all faith, so as to remove mountains, but do not have love, I am nothing. If I give away all my possessions, and if I hand over my body so that I may boast, but do not have love, I gain nothing.

Love is patient; love is kind; love is not envious or boastful or arrogant or rude. It does not insist on its own way; it is not irritable or resentful; it does not rejoice in wrongdoing, but rejoices in the truth. It bears all things, believes all things, hopes all things, endures all things.

Love never ends. But as for prophecies, they will come to an end; as for tongues, they will cease; as for knowledge, it will come to an end. For we know only in part, and we prophesy only in part; but when the complete comes, the partial will come to an end. When I was a child, I spoke like a child, I thought like a child, I reasoned like a child; when I became an adult, I put an end to childish ways. For now we see in a mirror, dimly, but then we will see face to face. Now I know only in part; then I will know fully, even as I have been fully known. And now faith, hope, and love abide, these three; and the greatest of these is love.

That Christ May Dwell in Your Hearts

EPHESIANS 3. 14-21

(Authorized Version)

For this cause I bow my knees unto the Father of our Lord Jesus Christ,

Of whom the whole family in heaven and earth is named,

That he would grant you, according to the riches of his glory, to be strengthened with might by his Spirit in the inner man;

That Christ may dwell in your hearts by faith; that ye, being rooted and grounded in love,

May be able to comprehend with all saints what is the breadth, and length, and depth, and height;

And to know the love of Christ, which passeth knowledge, that ye might be filled with all the fulness of God.

Now unto him that is able to do exceeding abundantly above all that we ask or think, according to the power that worketh in us.

Unto him be glory in the church by Christ Jesus throughout all ages, world without end.

Amen.

(New Revised Standard Version)

For this reason I bow my knees before the Father, from whom every family in heaven and on earth takes its name. I pray that, according to the riches of his glory, he may grant that you may be strengthened in your inner being with power through his Spirit, and that Christ may dwell in your hearts through faith, as you are being rooted and grounded in love. I pray that you may have the power to comprehend, with all the saints, what is the breadth and length and height and depth, and to know the love of Christ that surpasses knowledge, so that you may be filled with all the fullness of God.

Now to him who by the power at work within us is able to accomplish abundantly far more than all we can ask or imagine, to him be glory in the church and in Christ Jesus to all generations, for ever and ever. Amen.

Husbands and Wives

EPHESIANS 5. 17-33

(Authorized Version)

Wherefore be ye not unwise, but understanding what the will of he Lord is.

And be not drunk with wine, wherein is excess; but be filled with the Spirit;

Speaking to yourselves in psalms and hymns and spiritual songs, singing and making melody in your heart to the Lord;

Giving thanks always for all things unto God and the Father in the name of our Lord Jesus Christ;

Submitting yourselves one to another in the fear of God.

Wives, submit yourselves unto your own husbands, as unto the Lord.

For the husband is the head of the wife, even as Christ is the head of the church: and he is the saviour of the body.

Therefore as the church is subject unto Christ, so let the wives be to their own husbands in every thing.

Husbands, love your wives, even as Christ also loved the church, and gave himself for it;

That he might sanctify and cleanse it with the washing of water by the word.

That he might present it to himself a glorious church, not having spot, or wrinkle, or any such thing; but that it should be holy and without blemish.

So ought men to love their wives as their own bodies. He that loveth his wife loveth himself.

For no man ever yet hated his own flesh; but nourisheth and cherisheth it, even as the Lord the church:

For we are members of his body, of his flesh, and of his bones.

For this cause shall a man leave his father and mother, and shall be joined unto his wife, and they two shall be one flesh.

This is a great mystery: but I speak concerning Christ and the church.

Nevertheless let every one of you in particular so love his wife even as himself; and the wife see that she reverence her husband.

(New Revised Standard Version)

So do not be foolish, but understand what the will of the Lord is. Do not get drunk with wine, for that is debauchery; but be filled with the Spirit, as you sing psalms and hymns and spiritual songs among yourselves, singing and making melody to the Lord in your hearts, giving thanks to God the Father at all times and for everything in the name of our Lord Jesus Christ.

Be subject to one another out of reverence for Christ.

Wives, be subject to your husbands as you are to the Lord. For the husband is the head of the wife just as Christ is the head of the church, the body of which he is the Saviour. Just as the church is subject to Christ, so also wives ought to be, in everything, to their husbands.

Husbands, love your wives, just as Christ loved the church and gave himself up for her, in order to make her holy by cleansing her with the washing of water by the word, so as to present the church to himself in splendour, without a spot or wrinkle or anything of the kind – yes, so that she may be holy and without blemish. In the same way, husbands should love their wives as they do their own bodies. He who loves his wife loves himself. For no one ever hates his own body, but he nourishes and tenderly cares for it, just as Christ does for the church, because we are members of his body. 'For this reason a man will leave his father and mother and be joined to his wife, and the two will become one flesh.' This is a great mystery, and I am applying it to Christ and the church. Each of you, however, should love his wife as himself, and a wife should respect her husband.

The Peace of God

PHILIPPIANS 4. 4-9

(Authorized Version)

Rejoice in the Lord alway; and again I say, Rejoice.

Let your moderation be known unto all men. The Lord is at hand.

Be careful for nothing; but in every thing by prayer and supplication with thanksgiving let your requests be made known unto God.

And the peace of God, which passeth all understanding, shall keep your hearts and minds through Christ Jesus.

Finally, brethren, whatsoever things are true, whatsoever things are honest, whatsoever things are just, whatsoever things are pure, whatsoever things are lovely, whatsoever things are of good report; if there be any virtue, and if there be any praise, think on these things.

Those things, which ye have both learned, and received, and heard, and seen in me, do: and the God of peace shall be with you.

(New Revised Standard Version)

Rejoice in the Lord always; again I will say, Rejoice. Let your gentleness be known to everyone. The Lord is near. Do not worry about anything, but in everything by prayer and supplication with thanksgiving let your requests be made known to God. And the peace of God, which surpasses all understanding, will guard your hearts and your minds in Christ Jesus.

Finally, beloved, whatever is true, whatever is honourable, whatever is just, whatever is pure, whatever is pleasing, whatever is commendable, if there is any excellence and if there is anything worthy of praise, think about these things. Keep on doing the things that you have learned and received and heard and seen in me, and the God of peace will be with you.

Clothe Yourselves with Love

COLOSSIANS 3. 12-17

(Authorized Version)

Put on therefore, as the elect of God, holy and beloved, bowels of mercies, kindness, humbleness of mind, meekness, longsuffering;

Forbearing one another, and forgiving one another, if any man have a quarrel against any: even as Christ forgave you, so also do ye.

And above all these things put on charity, which is the bond of perfectness.

And let the peace of God rule in your hearts, to the which also ye are called in one body; and be ye thankful.

Let the word of Christ dwell in you richly in all wisdom; teaching and admonishing one another in psalms and hymns and spiritual songs, singing with grace in your hearts to the Lord.

And whatsoever ye do in word or deed, do all in the name of the Lord Jesus, giving thanks to God and the Father by him.

(New Revised Standard Version)

As God's chosen ones, holy and beloved, clothe yourselves with compassion, kindness, humility, meekness, and patience. Bear with one another and, if anyone has a complaint against another, forgive each other; just as the Lord has forgiven you, so you also must forgive. Above all, clothe yourselves with love, which binds everything together in perfect harmony. And let the peace of Christ rule in your hearts, to which indeed you were called in the one body. And be thankful. Let the word of Christ dwell in you richly; teach and admonish one another in all wisdom; and with gratitude in your hearts sing psalms, hymns, and spiritual songs to God. And whatever you do, in word or deed, do everything in the name of the Lord Jesus, giving thanks to God the Father through him.

Love in Deed and in Truth

I JOHN 3. 18-24

(Authorized Version)

My little children let us not love in word, neither in tongue; but in deed and in truth.

And hereby we know that we are of the truth, and shall assure our hearts before him.

For it our heart condemn us, God is greater than our heart, and knoweth all things.

Beloved, if our heart condemn us not, then have we confidence towards God.

And whatsoever we ask, we receive of him, because we keep his commandments, and do those things that are pleasing in his sight.

And this is his commandment, That we should believe on the name of his Son Jesus Christ, and love one another, as he gave us commandment.

And he that keepeth his commandments dwelleth in him, and he in him. And hereby we know that he abideth in us, by the Spirit which he hath given us.

(New Revised Standard Version)

Little children, let us love, not in word or speech, but in truth and action. And by this we will know that we are from the truth and will reassure our hearts before him whenever our hearts condemn us; for God is greater than our hearts, and he knows everything. Beloved, if our hearts do not condemn us, we have boldness before God; and we receive from him whatever we ask, because we obey his commandments and do what pleases him.

And this is his commandment, that we should believe in the name of his Son Jesus Christ and love one another, just as he has commanded us. All who obey his commandments abide in him, and he abides in them. And by this we know that he abides in us, by the Spirit that he has given us.

Love Is of God

I JOHN 4, 7-14

(Authorized Version)

Beloved, let us love one another: for love is of God; and every one that loveth is born of God, and knoweth God.

He that loveth not knoweth not God; for God is love.

In this was manifested the love of God toward us, because that God sent his only begotten Son into the world, that we might live through him.

Herein is love, not that we loved God, but that he loved us, and sent his Son to be the propitiation for our sins.

Beloved, if God so loved us, we ought also to love one another.

No man hath seen God at any time. If we love one another, God dwelleth in us, and his love is perfected in us.

Hereby know we that we dwell in him, and he in us, because he hath given us of his Spirit.

And we have seen and do testify that the Father sent the Son to be the Saviour of the world.

(New Revised Standard Version)

Beloved, let us love one another, because love is from God; everyone who loves is born of God and knows God. Whoever does not love does not know God, for God is love. God's love was revealed among us in this way: God sent his only Son into the world so that we might live through him. In this is love, not that we loved God but that he loved us and sent his Son to be the atoning sacrifice for our sins. Beloved, since God loved us so much, we also ought to love one another. No one has ever seen God; if we love one another, God lives in us, and his love is perfected in us.

By this we know that we abide in him and he in us, because he has given us of his Spirit. And we have seen and do testify that the Father has sent his Son as the Saviour of the world.

God Is Love

I JOHN 4. 15-21

(Authorized Version)

Whosoever shall confess that Jesus is the Son of God, God dwelleth in
him, and he in God.

And we have known and believed the love that God hath to us. God is
love; and he that dwelleth in love dwelleth in God, and God in him.

Herein is our love made perfect, that we may have boldness in the day
of judgment: because as he is, so are we in this world.

There is no fear in love; but perfect love casteth out fear: because fear
hath torment. He that feareth is not made perfect in love.

We love him, because he first loved us.

If a man say, I love God, and hateth his brother, he is a liar: for he that
loveth not his brother whom he hath seen, how can he love God
whom he hath not seen?

And this commandment have we from him, That he who loveth God
love his brother also.

(New Revised Standard Version)

God abides in those who confess that Jesus is the Son of God, and they
abide in God. So we have known and believe the love that God has for
us.

God is love, and those who abide in love abide in God, and God
abides in them. Love has been perfected among us in this: that we may
have boldness on the day of judgement, because as he is, so are we in
this world. There is no fear in love, but perfect love casts out fear; for
fear has to do with punishment, and whoever fears has not reached
perfection in love. We love because he first loved us. Those who say, 'I
love God', and hate their brothers or sisters, are liars; for those who do
not love a brother or sister whom they have seen, cannot love God
whom they have not seen. The commandment we have from him is
this: those who love God must love their brothers and sisters also.

The Marriage of the Lamb

REVELATION 19. 5-9

(Authorized Version)

And a voice came out of the throne, saying, Praise our God, all ye his servants, and ye that fear him, both small and great.

And I heard as it were the voice of a great multitude, and as the voice of many waters, and as the voice of mighty thunderings, saying, Alleluia: for the Lord God omnipotent reigneth.

Let us be glad and rejoice, and give honour to him: for the marriage of the Lamb is come, and his wife hath made herself ready.

And to her was granted that she should be arrayed in fine linen, clean and white: for the fine linen is the righteousness of saints.

And he saith unto me, Write, Blessed are they which are called unto the marriage supper of the Lamb. And he saith unto me, These are the true sayings of God.

(New Revised Standard Version)

And from the throne came a voice saying,

> 'Praise our God,
> all you his servants,
> and all who fear him,
> small and great.'

Then I heard what seemed to be the voice of a great multitude, like the sound of many waters and like the sound of mighty thunder-peals, crying out,

> 'Hallelujah!
> For the Lord our God
> the Almighty reigns.
> Let us rejoice and exult
> and give him the glory,
> for the marriage of the Lamb has come,

and his bride has made herself ready;
to her it has been granted to be clothed
with fine linen, bright and pure'
for the fine linen is the righteous deeds of the saints.

And the angel said to me, 'Write this: Blessed are those who are invited to the marriage supper of the Lamb.' And he said to me, 'These are true words of God.'

Poems and Reflections

The following quick guide will help you to choose readings for the type of wedding you have planned (for some of the constraints affecting church and civil weddings see the Introduction).

Readings that are *not* listed in one of the following categories should be equally suitable for each type of event.

Suitable for religious weddings:

Browning p. 73; Ford p. 97; Fuertes p. 99; Gibran p. 100; Gibran p. 101; Herbert p. 108; Hood p. 113; Hopkins p. 114; Law p. 122; Lawrence p. 124; Lewis p. 128; Quarles p. 147; Rumi p. 155; Taylor p. 171; Thomas à Kempis p. 176; Traherne p. 177; Vanstone p. 178; Weil p. 180

More suitable for civil weddings:

Abse p. 56; Ashford p. 64; Campion p. 77; Cope p. 82; Cuddon p. 83; Hannah p. 104; Henri p. 107; Laux p. 120; Lear p. 126; Logue p. 130; Nash p. 140; Patten p. 143; Patten p. 144; Russell p. 156

Particularly suitable for same-sex ceremonies:

Duffy p. 93; Matthew of Rievaulx p. 134; Whitman p. 181; Whitman p. 182

Suitable for those renewing vows or marrying a long-established partner:

Bishop p. 68; Blumenthal p. 69; Bradstreet p. 71; Burns p. 75; Cartwright p. 78; Carver p. 79; Crabbe p. 82; Drayton p. 90; Eliot p. 93; Fanthorpe p. 94; Fanthorpe p. 95; Lawrence p. 123; Lawrence p. 126; Lindbergh p. 129; Lowell p. 130; Nash p. 139; Ormond p. 141; Parker p. 143; Rilke p. 151; Stevenson p. 169; Tessimond p. 175; Wilson p. 183

Epithalamion

DANNIE ABSE
(Welsh; 1923–   )

Singing, today I married my white girl
beautiful in a barley field.
Green on thy finger a grass blade curled,
so with this ring I thee wed, I thee wed,
and send our love to the loveless world
of all the living and all the dead.

Now, no more than vulnerable human,
we, more than one, less than two,
are nearly ourselves in a barley field—
and only love is the rent that's due
though the bailiffs of time return anew
to all the living but not the dead.

Shipwrecked, the sun sinks down harbours
of a sky, unloads its liquid cargoes
of marigolds, and I and my white girl
lie still in the barley—who else wishes
to speak, what more can be said
by all the living against all the dead?

Come then all you wedding guests:
green ghost of trees, gold of barley,
you blackbird priests in the field,
you wind that shakes the pansy head
fluttering on a stalk like a butterfly;
come the living and come the dead.

Listen flowers, birds, winds, worlds,
tell all today that I married
more than a white girl in the barley—
for today I took to my human bed
flower and bird and wind and world,
and all the living and all the dead.

Love's Spaciousness

DIANE ACKERMAN

(American; 1956–   )

Love. What a small word we use for an idea so immense and powerful
it has altered the flow of history, calmed monsters, kindled works of
art, cheered the forlorn, turned tough guys to mush, consoled the
enslaved, driven strong women mad, glorified the humble, fueled
national scandals, bankrupted robber barons, and made mincemeat of
kings. How can love's spaciousness be conveyed in the narrow con-
fines of one syllable? Love is an ancient delirium, a desire older than
civilization, with taproots stretching deep into dark and mysterious
days…The heart is a living museum. In each of its galleries, no matter
how narrow or dimly lit, preserved forever like wondrous diatoms, are
our moments of loving and being loved.

From *A Natural History of Love*.

An Apache Blessing

ANONYMOUS

Now you will feel no rain,
for each of you will be a shelter to the other.

Now you will feel no cold,
for each of you will be warmth to the other.

Now there will be no loneliness,
for each of you will be a comfort to the other.

Now you are two persons,
but there is only one life before you.

Go now to your dwelling place,
to enter into the days of your togetherness.

And may your days be good
and long upon the earth.

Blessing for a Lover

ANONYMOUS

You are the star of each night,
You are the brightness of every morning,
You are the story of each guest,
You are the report of every land.

No evil shall befall you. On hill nor bank,
In field or valley. On mountain or in glen.

Neither above nor below. Neither in sea
   Nor on shore.
In skies above, nor in the depths.

You are the kernel of my heart,
You are the face of my sun,
You are the harp of my music,
You are the crown of my company.

Translated from the Scottish Gaelic by Caitlin Matthews.

When Two People Are at One

ANONYMOUS

When two people are at one
   in their inmost hearts
They shatter even the strength of iron
   or of bronze;
And when two people understand each other
   in their inmost hearts
Their words are sweet and strong
   like the fragrance of orchids.

From the *I Ching* (Chinese; 12th century BC).

Boundless Goodwill

ANONYMOUS

This is what should be done by the man and woman who are wise, who seek the good, and who know the meaning of the place of peace.

Let them be fervent, upright, and sincere, without conceit of self, easily contented and joyous, free of cares; let them not be submerged by the things of the world; let them not take upon themselves the burden of worldly goods; let their senses be controlled; let them be wise but not puffed up, and let them not desire great possessions even for their families. Let them do nothing that is mean or that the wise would reprove…

Even as a mother watches over and protects her child, her only child, so with a boundless mind should one cherish all living things, radiating friendliness over the entire world, above, below, and all around without limit. So let them cultivate a boundless goodwill toward the entire world, unlimited, free from ill-will or enmity.

Standing or walking, sitting or lying down, during all their waking hours, let them establish this mindfulness of goodwill, which is the highest state.

From the Buddhist scriptures (2nd–3rd century AD); translated from
the Pali by Edward Conze.

A Passionate Proposal

DAISY ASHFORD
(British; 1881–1972)

They arrived at Windsor very hot from the journey and Bernard at once hired a boat to row his beloved up the river. Ethel could not row but she much enjoyed seeing the tough sunburnt arms of Bernard tugging at the oars as she lay among the rich cushons of the dainty boat. She had a rarther lazy nature but Bernard did not know of this. However he soon got dog tired and suggested lunch by the mossy bank.

Oh yes said Ethel quickly opening the sparkling champaigne. Dont spill any cried Bernard as he carved some chicken.

They eat and drank deeply of the charming viands ending up with merangs and choclates.

Let us now bask under the spreading trees said Bernard in a passiunate tone.

Oh yes lets said Ethel and she opened her dainty parasole and sank down upon the long green grass. She closed her eyes but she was far from asleep. Bernard sat beside her in profound silence gazing at her pink face and long wavy eye lashes…

Ethel he murmered in a trembly voice.

Oh what is it said Ethel hastily sitting up.

Words fail me ejaculated Bernard horsly my passion for you is intense he added fervently. It has grown day and night since I first beheld you.

Oh said Ethel in supprise I am not prepared for this and she lent back against the trunk of the tree.

Bernard placed one arm tightly round her. When will you marry me Ethel he uttered you must be my wife it has come to that I love you so intensly that if you say no I shall perforce dash my body to the brink of yon muddy river he panted wildly.

Oh dont do that implored Ethel breathing rather hard.

Then say you love me he cried.

Oh Bernard she sighed fervently I certinly love you madly you are to me like a Heathen god she cried looking at his manly form and handsome flashing face I will indeed marry you.

How soon gasped Bernard gazing at her intensly.

As soon as possible said Ethel gently closing her eyes.

My Darling whispered Bernard and he seized her in his arms we will be marrid next week.

Oh Bernard muttered Ethel this is so sudden.

No no cried Bernard and taking the bull by both horns he kissed her violently on her dainty face. My bride to be he murmered several times.

Ethel trembled with joy as she heard the mistick words.

Oh Bernard she said little did I ever dream of such as this and she suddenly fainted into his out stretched arms.

Oh I say gasped Bernard and laying the dainty burden on the grass he dashed to the waters edge and got a cup full of the fragrant river to pour on his true loves pallid brow.

She soon came to and looked up with a sickly smile Take me back to the Gaierty hotel she whispered faintly.

From *The Young Visiters*, written when the author was nine years old.

Habitation

MARGARET ATWOOD
(Canadian; 1939–   )

Marriage is not
a house or even a tent

it is before that, and colder:

the edge of the forest, the edge
of the desert
               the unpainted stairs
at the back where we squat
outside, eating popcorn

the edge of the receding glacier

where painfully and with wonder
at having survived even
this far

we are learning to make fire

Carry Her Over the Water

W. H. AUDEN
(British; 1907–73)

Carry her over the water,
  And set her down under the tree,
Where the culvers white all day and all night,
  And the winds from every quarter,
Sing agreeably, agreeably, agreeably of love.

Put a gold ring on her finger,
  And press her close to your heart,
While the fish in the lake their snapshots take,
  And the frog, that sanguine singer,
Sings agreeably, agreeably, agreeably of love.

The streets shall all flock to your marriage,
  The houses turn around to look,
The tables and chairs say suitable prayers,
  And the horses drawing your carriage
Sing agreeably, agreeably, agreeably of love.

Married Happiness

A. C. BENSON
(British; 1862–1925)

A young husband and wife came to stay with us in all the first flush of married happiness. One realised all day long that other people merely made a pleasant background for their love, and that for each there was but one real figure on the scene. This was borne witness to by a whole armoury of gentle looks, swift glances, silent gestures. They were both full to the brim of a delicate laughter, of over-brimming wonder, of tranquil desire. And we all took a part in their gracious happiness…

These two spirits seemed, with hands intertwined, to have ascended gladly into the mountain, and to have seen a transfiguration of life: which left them not in a blissful eminence of isolation, but rather, as it were, beckoning others upwards, and saying that the road was indeed easy and plain…whatever might befall, they had tasted of the holy wine of joy, they had blessed the cup, and bidden us, too, to set our lips to it.

To His Wife on the Fourteenth Anniversary of Her Wedding Day, with a Ring

SAMUEL BISHOP
(British; 1731–95)

'Thee, Mary, with this ring I wed,'
So, fourteen years ago, I said.
Behold another ring! 'For what?'
To wed thee o'er again – why not?

With that first ring I married youth,
Grace, beauty, innocence, and truth;
Taste long admired, sense long revered,
And all my Molly then appeared.

If she, by merit since disclosed,
Prove twice the woman I supposed,
I plead that double merit now,
To justify a double vow.
Here then, today – with faith as sure,
With ardour as intense and pure,
As when amidst the rites divine
I took thy troth, and plighted mine –
To thee, sweet girl, my second ring,
A token, and a pledge, I bring;

With this I wed, till death us part,
Thy riper virtues to my heart;
Those virtues which, before untried,
The wife has added to the bride –
Those virtues, whose progressive claim,
Endearing wedlock's very name,
My soul enjoys, my song approves,
For conscience' sake as well as love's.

For why? – They show me every hour
Honour's high thought, affection's power,
Discretion's deed, sound judgment's sentence,
And teach me all things – but repentance.

A Marriage

MICHAEL BLUMENTHAL
(American; 1949–   )

You are holding up a ceiling
with both arms. It is very heavy,
but you must hold it up, or else
it will fall down on you. Your arms
are tired, terribly tired,
and, as the day goes on, it feels
as if either your arms or the ceiling
will soon collapse.

But then,
unexpectedly,
something wonderful happens:

Someone,
a man or a woman,
walks into the room
and holds their arms up
to the ceiling beside you.

So you finally get
to take down your arms.
You feel the relief of respite,
the blood flowing back
to your fingers and arms.
And when your partner's arms tire,
you hold up your own
to relieve him again.

And it can go on like this
for many years
without the house falling.

Such Different Wants

ROBERT BLY
(American; 1926–   )

The board floats on the river.
The board wants nothing
but is pulled from beneath
on into deeper waters.

And the elephant dwelling
on the mountain wants
a trumpet so its dying cry
can be heard by the stars.

The wakeful heron striding
through reeds at dawn wants
the god of sun and moon
to see his long skinny neck.

You must say what you want.
I want to be the man
and I am who will love you
when your hair is white.

To My Dear and Loving Husband

ANNE BRADSTREET
(American; c. 1612–72)

If ever two were one, then surely we.
If ever man were loved by wife, then thee:
If ever wife was happy in a man,
Compare with me ye women if you can.
I prize thy love more than whole mines of gold,
Or all the riches that the Earth dost hold.

My love is such that rivers cannot quench,
Nor ought but love from thee, give recompense.
Thy love is such I can no way repay,
The heavens reward thee manifold I pray.
Then while we live, in love let's so persever,
That when we live no more, we may live ever.

Because She Would Ask Me Why I Loved Her

CHRISTOPHER BRENNAN
(Australian; 1870–1932)

If questioning could make us wise
no eyes would ever gaze in eyes;
if all our tale were told in speech
no mouths would wander each to each.

Were spirits free from mortal mesh
and love not bound in hearts of flesh
no aching breasts would yearn to meet
and find their ecstasy complete.

For who is there that lives and knows
the secret powers by which he grows?
were knowledge all, what were our need
to thrill and faint and sweetly bleed?

Then seek not, sweet, the *If* and *Why*
I love you now until I die:
For I must love because I live
And life in me is what you give.

How Do I Love Thee? Let Me Count the Ways

ELIZABETH BARRETT BROWNING
(British; 1806–61)

How do I love thee? Let me count the ways.
I love thee to the depth and breadth and height
My soul can reach, when feeling out of sight
For the ends of being and ideal grace.
I love thee to the level of every day's
Most quiet need, by sun and candlelight.
I love thee freely, as men strive for right;
I love thee purely, as they turn from praise.
I love thee with the passion put to use
In my old griefs, and with my childhood's faith.
I love thee with a love I seemed to lose
With my lost saints – I love thee with the breath,
Smiles, tears, of all my life! – and, if God choose,
I shall but love thee better after death.

From *Sonnets from the Portuguese*.

If Thou Must Love Me

ELIZABETH BARRETT BROWNING
(British; 1806–61)

If thou must love me, let it be for naught
Except for love's sake only. Do not say

'I love her for her smile – her look – her way
Of speaking gently, – for a trick of thought
That falls in well with mine, and certes brought
A sense of pleasant ease on such a day' –
For these things in themselves, Beloved, may
Be changed, or change for thee – and love, so wrought,
May be unwrought so. Neither love me for
Thine own dear pity's wiping my cheeks dry:
A creature might forget to weep, who bore
Thy comfort long, and lose thy love thereby!
But love me for love's sake, that evermore
Thou mayst love on, through love's eternity.

From *Sonnets from the Portuguese.*

John Anderson My Jo

ROBERT BURNS
(Scottish; 1759–96)

John Anderson my jo, John,
      When we were first acquent,
Your locks were like the raven,
      Your bonnie brow was brent;
But now your brow is beld, John,
      Your locks are like the snow;
But blessings on your frosty pow,
      John Anderson, my jo.

John Anderson my jo, John,
      We clamb the hill thegither;

And mony a canty day, John,
    We've had wi ane anither:
Now we maun totter down, John,
    And hand in hand we'll go,
And sleep thegither at the foot,
    John Anderson, my jo.

A Red, Red Rose

ROBERT BURNS
(Scottish; 1759–96)

My love is like a red, red rose
    That's newly sprung in June:
My love is like the melody
    That's sweetly played in tune.

As fair art thou, my bonnie lass,
    So deep in love am I:
And I will love thee still, my dear,
    Till a' the seas gang dry.

Till a' the seas gang dry, my dear,
    And the rocks melt wi' the sun:
And I will love thee still, my dear,
    While the sands o' life shall run.

And fare thee weel, my only love,
    And fare thee weel a while!
And I will come again, my love,
    Thou' it were ten thousand mile.

She Walks in Beauty

GEORGE GORDON NOEL, LORD BYRON
(British; 1788–1824)

She walks in beauty, like the night
　　Of cloudless climes and starry skies;
And all that's best of dark and bright
　　Meet in her aspect and her eyes:
Thus mellowed to that tender light
　　Which heaven to gaudy day denies.

One shade the more, one ray the less,
　　Had half impaired the nameless grace,
Which waves in every raven tress,
　　Or softly lightens o'er her face;
Where thoughts serenely sweet express
　　How pure, how dear their dwelling-place.

And on that cheek, and o'er that brow,
　　So soft, so calm, yet eloquent,
The smiles that win, the tints that glow,
　　But tell of days in goodness spent,
A mind at peace with all below,
　　A heart whose love is innocent.

My Sweetest Lesbia

THOMAS CAMPION
(English; 1567–1620)

My sweetest Lesbia, let us live and love;
And, though the sager sort our deeds reprove,
Let us not weigh them. Heaven's great lamps do dive
Into their west, and straight again revive.
But soon as once set is our little light,
Then must we sleep one ever-during night.

If all would lead their lives in love like me,
Then bloody swords and armour should not be;
No drum nor trumpet peaceful sleeps should move,
Unless alarm came from the camp of Love.
But fools do live and waste their little light,
And seek with pain their ever-during night.

When timely death my life and fortune ends,
Let not my hearse be vexed with mourning friends
But let all lovers, rich in triumph, come
And with sweet pastimes grace my happy tomb.
And, Lesbia, close up thou my little light,
And crown with love my ever-during night.

To Chloe, Who for His Sake Wished Herself Younger

WILLIAM CARTWRIGHT
(English; 1611–43)

There are two births; the one when light
    First strikes the new awakened sense;
The other when two souls unite,
    And we must count our life from thence:
When you loved me and I loved you
    Then both of us were born anew.

Love then to us new souls did give
    And in those souls did plant new powers;
Since when another life we live,
    The breath we breathe is his, not ours:
Love makes those young whom age doth chill,
    And whom he finds young keeps young still.

Late Fragment

RAYMOND CARVER
(American; 1939–88)

And did you get what
you wanted from this life, even so?
I did.
And what did you want?
To call myself beloved, to feel myself
beloved on the earth.

For a Wedding

KATE CLANCHY
(British; 1965–   )

Cousin, I think the shape of a marriage
is like the shelves my parents have carried
through Scotland to London, three houses;

is not distinguished, fine, French-polished,
but plywood and tatty, made
in the first place for children to batter,

still carrying markings in green felt-tip,
but always, where there are books
and a landing, managing to fit;

that marriage has lumps like
their button-backed sofa, constantly,
shortly, about to be stuffed;

and that love grows fat
as their squinting cat, swelling
round as a loaf from her basket.

I wish you years that shape, that form,
and a pond in a Sunday, urban garden;
where you'll see your joined reflection tremble,

stand and watch the waterboatmen
skate with ease across the surface tension.

Patagonia

KATE CLANCHY
(British; 1965–   )

I said *perhaps Patagonia*, and pictured
a peninsula, wide enough
for a couple of ladderback chairs
to wobble on at high tide. I thought

of us in breathless cold, facing
a horizon round as a coin, looped
in a cat's cradle strung by gulls
from sea to sun. I planned to wait

till the waves had bored themselves
to sleep, till the last clinging barnacles,
growing worried in the hush, had
paddled off in tiny coracles, till

those restless birds, your actor's hands,
had dropped slack into your lap,
until you'd turned, at last, to me.
When I spoke of Patagonia, I meant

skies all empty aching blue. I meant
years. I meant all of them with you.

Fragment from a Notebook

SAMUEL TAYLOR COLERIDGE
(British; 1772–1834)

And in Life's noisiest hour,
There whispers still the ceaseless Love of Thee,
The heart's *Self-solace* and soliloquy.

You mould my hopes, you fashion me within;
And to the leading Love-throb in the Heart
Thro' all my Being all my pulses beat.
You lie in all my many Thoughts, like Light,
Like the fair light of Dawn, or summer-Eve
On rippling Stream, or cloud-reflecting Lake.

And looking to the Heaven, that bends above you
How oft I bless the Lot, that made me love you.

Giving Up Smoking

WENDY COPE
(British; 1945–   )

There's not a Shakespeare sonnet
Or a Beethoven quartet
That's easier to like than you
Or harder to forget.

You think that sounds extravagant?
I haven't finished yet –
I like you more than I would like
To have a cigarette.

A Marriage Ring

GEORGE CRABBE
(British; 1754–1832)

The ring so worn, as you behold,
    So thin, so pale, is yet of gold:
The passion such it was to prove;
Worn with life's cares, love yet was love.

I'll Be There

LOUISE CUDDON
(British; 1971–   )

I'll be there, my darling,
Through thick and through thin
When your mind is a mess
When your head's in a spin
When your plane's been delayed
When you've missed the last train
When life is just threatening
To drive you insane
When your thrilling whodunnit
Has lost its last page
When somebody tells you
You're looking your age
When your coffee's too cool
And your wine is too warm
When the forecast said 'Fine'
But you're out in a storm
When you ordered the korma
But got the Madras
When you wake in the night
And are sure you smell gas
When your quick-break hotel
Is more like a slum
And your holiday photos
Show only your thumb
When you park for five minutes
In a residents' bay
And return to discover
You've been towed away
When the jeans that you bought

In hope or in haste
Stick to your hips
And won't reach round your waist
When the dentist looks into
Your mouth and just sighs
When your heroes turn out
To be wimps in disguise
When the food you most like
Brings you out in red rashes
When as soon as you boot up
The bloody thing crashes
When you're in extra time
And the other team scores
When someone informs you
There's no Santa Claus
When you gaze at the stars
And step on a nail
When you know you'll succeed
But, somehow, you fail
When your horoscope tells you
You'll have a good day
So you ask for a rise
And your boss says, 'No way.'
So my darling, my sweetheart, my dear…

When you spill your beer
When you shed a tear
When you burn the toast
When you miss the post
When you lose the plot
When I'm all you've got
When you break a rule
When you act the fool
When you've got the flu
When you're in a stew

When you're last in the queue
Don't feel blue
'Cause I'm telling you
I'll be there
    I'll be there
        I'll be there for you.

Love Is What We Need

A. POWELL DAVIES
(American; 1902–57)

When two individuals meet, so do two private worlds. None of our private worlds is big enough so that we could live a wholesome life in it alone. We need the wider world of joy and wonder, of purpose and venture, of toil and tears. What are we, any of us, but strangers and sojourners forlornly answering through the night time, until we draw together and find the meaning of our lives in one another, dissolving our fears in each other's courage, making music together, and lighting torches to guide us through the dark night? We belong together. Love is what we need, to love and to be loved. Let our hearts be open; and what we would receive from others let us give. For what is given still remains to bless the giver – when the gift is love.

Love Song

MARY CAROLYN DAVIES
(American; late 19th – early 20th century)

There is a strong wall about me to protect me:
It is built of the words you have said to me.

There are swords about me to keep me safe:
They are the kisses of your lips.

Before me goes a shield to guard me from harm:
It is the shadow of your arms between me and danger.

All the wishes of my mind know your name,
And the white desires of my heart
They are acquainted with you.
The cry of my body for completeness,
That is a cry to you.
My blood beats our your name to me, unceasing, pitiless
Your name, your name.

One Tree and Not Two

LOUIS DE BERNIÈRES
(British; 1954–   )

Love is a temporary madness, it erupts like volcanoes and then subsides. And when it subsides you have to make a decision. You have to work out whether your roots have so entwined together that it is inconceivable that you should ever part. Because this is what love is.

Love is not breathlessness, it is not excitement, it is not the promulgation of eternal passion. That is just being 'in love' which any fool can do. Love itself is what is left over when being in love has burned away, and this is both art and a fortunate accident. Those that truly love, have roots that grow towards each other underground and when all the pretty blossom has fallen from their branches, they find that they are one tree and not two.

From *Captain Corelli's Mandolin*.

The Present

MICHAEL DONAGHY
(American; 1954–2004)

For the present there is just one moon,
though every level pond gives back another.

But the bright disc shining in the black lagoon,
perceived by astrophysicist and lover,

is milliseconds old. And even that light's
seven minutes older than its source.

And the stars we think we see on moonless nights
are long extinguished. And, of course,

this very moment, as you read this line,
is literally gone before you know it.

Forget the here-and-now. We have no time
but this device of wantonness and wit.

Make me this present then: your hand in mine,
and we'll live out our lives in it.

The Good Morrow

JOHN DONNE
(English; 1572–1631)

I wonder by my troth, what thou and I
Did, till we loved? were we not weaned till then?
But sucked on country pleasures, childishly?
Or snorted we in the seven sleepers' den?
'Twas so; but this, all pleasures fancies be.
If ever any beauty I did see,
Which I desired, and got, 'twas but a dream of thee.

And now good morrow to our waking souls,
Which watch not one another out of fear;
For love, all love of other sights controls,
And makes one little room, an everywhere.
Let sea-discoverers to new worlds have gone,
Let maps to other, worlds on worlds have shown,
Let us possess one world, each hath one, and is one.

My face in thine eye, thine in mine appears,
And true plain hearts do in the faces rest;
Where can we find two better hemispheres
Without sharp North, without declining West?
What ever dies, was not mixed equally;
If our two loves be one, or thou and I
Love so alike that none do slacken, none can die.

The Sun Rising

JOHN DONNE
(English; 1572–1631)

Busy old fool, unruly sun,
Why dost thou thus,
Through windows, and through curtains call on us?
Must to thy motions lovers' seasons run?
Saucy pedantic wretch, go chide
Late school-boys, and sour prentices,
Go tell court-huntsmen, that the King will ride,
Call country ants to harvest offices;
Love, all alike, no season knows, nor clime,
Nor hours, days, months, which are the rags of time.

Thy beams, so reverend, and strong
Why shouldst thou think?
I could eclipse and cloud them with a wink,
But that I would not lose her sight so long:
If her eyes have not blinded thine,
Look, and tomorrow late, tell me,
Whether both th'Indias of spice and mine

Be where thou left'st them, or lie here with me.
Ask for those kings whom thou saw'st yesterday,
And thou shall hear, All here in one bed lay.

She's all states, and all princes, I,
Nothing else is.
Princes do but play us; compared to this,
All honour's mimic; all wealth alchemy.
Thou sun art half as happy as we,
In that the world's contracted thus;
Thine age asks ease, and since thy duties be
To warm the world, that's done in warming us.
Shine here to us, and thou art everywhere;
This bed thy centre is, these walls, thy sphere.

Verses Made the Night before He Died

MICHAEL DRAYTON
(English; 1563–1631)

So well I love thee as without thee I
Love nothing; if I might choose, I'd rather die
Than be one day debarred thy company.

Since beasts and plants do grow and live and move,
Beasts are those men that such a life approve:
He only lives that deadly is in love.

The corn, that in the ground is sown, first dies,
And of one seed do many ears arise;
Love, this world's corn, by dying multiplies.

The seeds of love first by thy eyes were thrown
Into a ground untilled, a heart unknown
To bear such fruit, til by thy hands `twas sown.

Look as your looking-glass by chance may fall,
Divide, and break in many pieces small,
And yet shows forth the selfsame face in all,

Proportions, features, graces, just the same,
And in the smallest piece as well the name
Of fairest one deserves as in the richest frame;

So all my thoughts are pieces but of you,
Which put together makes a glass so true
As I therein no other's face but yours can view.

Valentine

CAROL ANN DUFFY
(British; 1955–   )

Not a red rose or a satin heart.

I give you an onion.
It is a moon wrapped in brown paper.
It promises light
like the careful undressing of love.

Here.
It will blind you with tears
like a lover.

It will make your reflection
a wobbling photo of grief.

I am trying to be truthful.

Not a cute card or a kissogram.

I give you an onion.
Its fierce kiss will stay on your lips,
possessive and faithful
as we are,
for as long as we are.

Take it.
Its platinum loops shrink to a wedding-ring,
if you like.
Lethal.
Its scent will cling to your fingers,
cling to your knife.

White Writing

CAROL ANN DUFFY
(British; 1955–   )

No vows written to wed you,
I write them white,
my lips on yours,
light in the soft hours of our married years.

No prayers written to bless you,
I write them white,
your soul a flame,
bright in the window of your maiden name.

No laws written to guard you,
I write them white,
your hand in mine,
palm against palm, lifeline, heartline.

No rules written to guide you,
I write them white,
words on the wind,
traced with a stick where we walk on the sand.

No news written to tell you,
I write it white,
foam on a wave
as we lift up our skirts in the sea, wade,

see last gold sun behind clouds,
inked water in moonlight.
No poems written to praise you,
I write them white.

One With Each Other

GEORGE ELIOT
(British; 1819–80)

What greater thing is there for two human souls, than to feel they are joined for life – to strengthen each other in all labour, to rest on each other in all sorrow, to minister to each other in all pain, to be one with each other in silent unspeakable memories.

From *Adam Bede.*

A Dedication to My Wife

T. S. ELIOT
(Anglo-American; 1888–1965)

To whom I owe the leaping delight
That quickens my senses in our wakingtime
And the rhythm that governs the repose of our sleepingtime,
    The breathing in unison

Of lovers whose bodies smell of each other
Who think the same thoughts without need of speech
And babble the same speech without need of meaning.

No peevish winter wind shall chill
No sullen tropic sun shall wither
The roses in the rose-garden which is ours and ours only

But this dedication is for others to read:
These are private words addressed to you in public.

Atlas

U. A. FANTHORPE
(British; 1929–   )

There is a kind of love called maintenance,
Which stores the WD40 and knows when to use it;

Which checks the insurance, and doesn't forget
The milkman; which remembers to plant bulbs;

Which answers letters; which knows the way
The money goes; which deals with dentists

And Road Fund Tax and meeting trains,
And postcards to the lonely; which upholds

The permanently ricketty elaborate
Structures of living; which is Atlas.

And maintenance is the sensible side of love,
Which knows what time and weather are doing
To my brickwork; insulates my faulty wiring;
Laughs at my dryrotten jokes; remembers
My need for gloss and grouting; which keeps
My suspect edifice upright in air,
As Atlas did the sky.

7301

U. A. FANTHORPE
(British; 1929–   )

Learning to read you, twenty years ago,
Over the pub lunch cheese-and-onion rolls.

Learning you eat raw onions; learning your taste
For obscurity, how you encoded teachers and classrooms

As the hands, the shop-floor; learning to hide
The sudden shining naked looks of love. And thinking

The rest of our lives, the rest of our lives
Doing perfectly ordinary things together – riding

In buses, walking in Sainsbury's, sitting
In pubs eating cheese-and-onion rolls,

All those tomorrows. Now twenty years after,
We've had seventy-three hundred of them, and

(If your arithmetic's right, and our luck) we may
Fairly reckon on seventy-three hundred more.

I hold them crammed in my arms, colossal crops
Of shining tomorrows that may never happen.

But may they! Still learning to read you.
To hear what it is you're saying, to master the code.

Hinterhof

JAMES FENTON

(British; 1949-)

Stay near to me and I'll stay near to you –
As near as you are dear to me will do,
    Near as the rainbow to the rain,
    The west wind to the windowpane,
As fire to the hearth, as dawn to dew.

Stay true to me and I'll stay true to you –
As true as you are new to me will do,
    New as the rainbow in the spray,
    Utterly new in every way,
New in the way that what you say is true.

Stay near to me, stay true to me. I'll stay
As near, as true to you as heart could pray.
    Heart never hoped that one might be
    Half of the things you are to me –
The dawn, the fire, the rainbow and the day.

A Bridal Song

JOHN FORD
(English; 1586– c. 1640)

Comforts lasting, loves increasing,
Like soft hours never ceasing:
Plenty's pleasure, peace complying,
Without jars, or tongues envying;
Hearts by holy union wedded,
More than theirs by custom bedded;
Fruitful issues; life so gracèd,
Not by age to be defacèd,
Budding, as the year ensu'th,
Every spring another youth:
All what thought can add beside
Crown this bridegroom and this bride!

From *The Broken Heart*.

What It Is

ERICH FRIED
(Austrian; 1921–88)

It is madness
says reason
It is what it is
says love

It is unhappiness
says caution
It is nothing but pain
says fear
It has no future
says insight
It is what it is
says love

It is ridiculous
says pride
It is foolish
says caution
It is impossible
says experience
It is what it is
says love

Translated from the German by Stuart Hood.

When I Hear Your Name

GLORIA FUERTES
(Spanish; 1918–98)

When I hear your name
I feel a little robbed of it;
it seems unbelievable
that half a dozen letters could say so much.

My compulsion is to blast down every wall with your name,
I'd paint it on all the houses,
there wouldn't be a well
I hadn't leaned into
to shout your name there,
nor a stone mountain
where I hadn't uttered
those six separate letters
that are echoed back.

My compulsion is
to teach the birds to sing it,
to teach the fish to drink it,
to teach men that there is nothing
like the madness of repeating your name.

My compulsion is to forget altogether
the other 22 letters, all the numbers,
the books I've read, the poems I've written.
To say hello with your name.
To beg bread with your name.
'She always says the same thing,' they'd say when they saw me,
and I'd be so proud, so happy, so self-contained.

And I'll go to the other world with your name on my tongue,
and all the questions I'll answer with your name

– the judges and saints will understand nothing –
God will sentence me to repeating it endlessly and forever.

Translated from the Spanish by Philip Levine and Ada Long.

Over the Hills and Far Away

JOHN GAY
(British; 1685–1782)

Were I laid on Greenland's coast,
   And in my arms embraced my lass;
Warm amidst eternal frost,
Too soon the half year's night would pass.
Were I sold on Indian soil,
   Soon as the burning day was closed,
I could mock the sultry toil
   When on my charmer's breast reposed.
And I would love you all the day,
Every night would kiss and play,
If with me you'd fondly stray
Over the hills and far away.

From *The Beggar's Opera*.

Stand Together yet Not Too Near Together

KHALIL GIBRAN
(Lebanese-American; 1883–1931)

You were born together, and together you shall be for evermore.
You shall be together when the white wings of death scatter your days.
Aye, you shall be together even in the silent memory of God.
But let there be spaces in your togetherness,
And let the winds of the heavens dance between you.
Love one another but make not a bond of love:
Let it rather be a moving sea between the shores of your souls.
Fill each other's cup but drink not from one cup.
Give one another of your bread but eat not from the same loaf.
Sing and dance together and be joyous, but let each one of you be alone,
Even as the strings of a lute are alone though they quiver with the same music.
Give your hearts, but not into each other's keeping.
For only the hand of Life can contain your hearts.
And stand together yet not too near together:
For the pillars of the temple stand apart,
And the oak tree and cypress grow not in each other's shadow.

From *The Prophet*.

On Love

KHALIL GIBRAN
(Lebanese-American; 1883–1931)

When you love, you should not say, 'God is in my heart,' but rather, 'I am in the heart of God.'
And think not you can direct the course of love, for love, if it finds you worthy, directs your course.

Love has no other desire but to fulfill itself.
But if you love and must needs have desires, let these be your desires:
To melt and be like a running brook that sings its melody to the night.
To know the pain of too much tenderness.
To be wounded by your own understanding of love;
And to bleed willingly and joyfully.
To wake at dawn with a winged heart and give thanks for another day of loving;
To rest at the noon hour and meditate love's ecstasy;
To return home at eventide with gratitude;
And then to sleep with a prayer for the beloved in your heart and a song of praise upon your lips.

From *The Prophet*.

A Slice of Wedding Cake

ROBERT GRAVES
(British; 1895–1985)

Why have such scores of lovely, gifted girls
Married impossible men?
Simple self-sacrifice may be ruled out,
And missionary endeavour, nine times out of ten.

Repeat 'impossible men': not merely rustic,
Foul-tempered or depraved
(Dramatic foils chosen to show the world
How well women behave, and always have behaved).

Impossible men: idle, illiterate,
Self-pitying, dirty, sly,
For whose appearance even in City parks
Excuses must be made to casual passers-by.

Has God's supply of tolerable husbands
Fallen, in fact, so low?
Or do I always over-value woman
At the expense of man?
                    Do I?
                            It might be so.

Match

SOPHIE HANNAH
(British; 1971–   )

Love has not made us good.
We still do all the cynics said we would –
Struggle like heroes searching for a war,
Still want too much, and more.

Love has not made us nice.
Elders and betters with their best advice
Can't stir us from the lounger by the pool.
We dodge all work like school,

Leave urgent debts unpaid,
Cancel the solemn promises we've made
If loyalties or circumstances change.
Our thoughts are no less strange,

But love has made us last.
We do together all that in the past
We did alone; err not as one but two
And this is how I knew.

Whenever You Look Up

THOMAS HARDY
(British; 1840–1928)

'Come,' said Gabriel, freshening again; 'think a minute or two. I'll wait a while, Miss Everdene. Will you marry me? Do, Bathsheba. I love you far more than common!'

'I'll try to think,' she observed, rather more timorously; 'if I can think out of doors; my mind spreads away so.'

'But you can give a guess.'

'Then give me time.' Bathsheba looked thoughtfully into the distance, away from the direction in which Gabriel stood.

'I can make you happy,' said he to the back of her head…'You shall have a piano in a year or two – farmers' wives are getting to have pianos now – and I'll practise up the flute right well to play with you in the evenings.'

'Yes; I should like that.'

'And have one of those little ten-pound gigs for market – and nice flowers, and birds – cocks and hens I mean, because they be useful,' continued Gabriel, feeling balanced between poetry and practicality.

'I should like it very much.'

'And a frame for cucumbers – like a gentleman and lady.'

'Yes.'

'And when the wedding was over, we'd have it put in the newspaper list of marriages.'

'Dearly I should like that!'

'And the babies in the births – every man jack of 'em! And at home by the fire, whenever you look up, there I shall be – and whenever I look up there will be you.'

…

'Oh Mr Oak – that's very fine! You'd get to despise me.'

'Never,' said Mr Oak, so earnestly that he seemed to be coming, by the force of his words, straight through the bush and into her arms. 'I shall do one thing in this life – one thing certain – that is, love you, and long for you and KEEP WANTING YOU till I die.' His voice had a genuine pathos now, and his large brown hands perceptibly trembled.

From *Far from the Madding Crowd*.

Perfect Love

WILLIAM HAZLITT
(British; 1778–1830)

Perfect love has this advantage in it, that it leaves the possessor of it nothing further to desire. There is one object (at least) in which the soul finds absolute content, for which it seeks to live, or dares to die. The heart has as it were filled up the moulds of the imagination. The truth of passion keeps pace with and outvies the extravagance of mere language. There are no words so fine, no flattery so soft, that there is not a sentiment beyond them, that it is impossible to express at the bottom of the heart where true love is. What idle sounds the common phrases, *adorable creature*, *angel*, *divinity*, are! What a proud reflection it is to have a feeling answering to all these, rooted in the breast, unalterable, unutterable, to which all other feelings are light and vain! Perfect love reposes on the subject of its choice, like the halcyon on the wave; and the air of heaven is around it.

From *Liber Amoris*.

Love Is

ADRIEN HENRI
(British; 1932–2000)

Love is feeling cold in the back of vans
Love is a fanclub with only two fans
Love is walking holding painstained hands
Love is

Love is fish and chips on winter nights
Love is blankets full of strange delights
Love is when you don't put out the light
Love is

Love is the presents in Christmas shops
Love is when you're feeling Top of the Pops
Love is what happens when the music stops
Love is

Love is white panties lying all forlorn
Love is a pink nightdress still slightly warm
Love is when you have to leave at dawn
Love is

Love is you and love is me
Love is a prison and love is free
Love's what's there when you're away from me
Love is…

Love

GEORGE HERBERT
(English; 1593–1633)

Love bade me welcome; yet my soul drew back,
      Guilty of dust and sin.
But quick-eyed Love, observing me grow slack
      From my first entrance in,
Drew nearer to me, sweetly questioning,
      If I lacked anything.

'A guest', I answered, 'worthy to be here.'
      Love said, 'You shall be he.'
'I, the unkind, ungrateful? Ah, my dear,
      I cannot look on thee.'
Love took my hand, and smiling did reply,
      'Who made the eyes but I?'

'Truth, Lord, but I have marred them; let my shame
      Go where it doth deserve.'
'And know you not', says Love, 'who bore the blame?'
      'My dear, then I will serve.'
'You must sit down', says Love, 'and taste my meat.'
      So I did sit and eat.

A Ring Presented to Julia

ROBERT HERRICK
(English; 1591–1674)

Julia, I bring
To thee this ring,
Made for thy finger fit;
To show by this
That our love is
(Or should be) like to it.

Close though it be
The joint is free;
So, when love's yoke is on,
It must not gall,
Or fret at all
With hard oppression.

But it must play
Still either way,
And be, too, such a yoke
As not too wide
To overslide,
Or be so strait to choke.

So we who bear
This beam must rear
Ourselves to such a height
As that the stay
Of either may
Create the burden light.

And as this round
Is nowhere found
To flaw, or else to sever:
So let our love
As endless prove,
And pure as gold for ever.

To the Virgins, to Make Much of Time

ROBERT HERRICK
(English; 1591–1674)

Gather ye rosebuds while ye may,
Old Time is still a-flying:
And this same flower that smiles today
Tomorrow will be dying.

The glorious lamp of heaven, the sun,
The higher he's a-getting,
The sooner will his race be run,
And nearer he's to setting.

That age is best which is the first,
When youth and blood are warmer;
But being spent, the worse, and worst
Times, still succeed the former.

Then be not coy, but use your time:
And while ye may, go marry;
For having lost but once your prime,
You may for ever tarry.

24 September 1945

NAZIM HIKMET
(Turkish; 1901–63)

The best sea: has yet to be crossed.
The best child: has yet to be born.
The best days: have yet to be lived;
and the best word that I wanted to say to you
is the word that I have not yet said.

Translated from the Turkish by Richard McKane; one of a series of poems written to
his wife from prison.

They Are a Tableau at the Kissing-Gate

JANE HOLLAND
(British; 1966–   )

Maids of honour, bridegroom, bride,
the best man in a grey silk suit,
a flash to catch them in the arching
stone, confettied by a sudden gust –
an apple-tree in full white spread
beyond the reach of bone and dust.

I am the driver in a passing car:
the wedding-dress a cloud of lace.
A small hand clutching at a skirt,
some nervous bridesmaid, eight
or maybe nine years old, has seen
the blossom fall, has closed her eyes –

her head falls back into the scent,
the soundless whirr and whirl of earth-
bound petals, like sycamore seeds
on a current of air, silent helicopters
bringing light – a wedding-gift
the bride will brush away, unconsciously.

This is no ordinary act, no summer fête,
another simple wedding held in June.
This is the wind shaking the apple-tree,
the bell above the kissing-gate,
the sudden fall of blossom into light
which only love and innocence can see.

We must be held accountable to love:
where they step out together arm in arm
as newly-weds, spring-cleaned, and climb
into a waiting car beneath a summer sky,
the blossom will still fall, unstoppable –
a drift of change across a changeless time.

Ruth

THOMAS HOOD
(British; 1799–1845)

She stood breast high amid the corn,
Clasped by the golden light of morn,
Like the sweetheart of the sun,
Who many a glowing kiss had won.

On her cheek an autumn flush,
Deeply ripened; – such a blush
In the midst of brown was born,
Like red poppies grown with corn.

Round her eyes her tresses fell,
Which were blackest none could tell,
But long lashes veiled a light,
That had else been all too bright.

And her hat, with shady brim,
Made her tressy forehead dim; –
Thus she stood amid the stooks,
Praising God with sweetest looks; –

Sure, I said, heaven did not mean,
Where I reap thou shouldst but glean,
Lay thy sheaf adown and come,
Share my harvest and my home.

At the Wedding March

GERARD MANLEY HOPKINS
(British; 1844–89)

God with honour hang your head,
Groom, and grace you, bride, your bed
With lissome scions, sweet scions,
Out of hallowed bodies bred.

Each be other's comfort kind:
Deep, deeper than divined,
Divine charity, dear charity,
Fast you ever, fast bind.

Then let the March tread our ears:
I to Him turn with tears
Who to wedlock, his wonder wedlock,
Deals triumph and immortal years.

The Arduous Drama of Staying in Love

MICHAEL IGNATIEFF
(Canadian; 1947–   )

In the marriage ceremony, that moment of falling in love is replaced
by the arduous drama of staying in love, the words 'in sickness and in
health, for richer, for poorer, till death us do part' set love in the temporal context in which it achieves its meaning. As time begins to

elapse, one begins to love the other because they have shared the same experience…Selves may not intertwine; but lives do, and shared memory becomes as much of a bond as the bond of the flesh.

From *Lodged in the Heart and Memory*.

Tell Me

ELIZABETH JENNINGS
(British; 1926–2001)

Tell me where you go
When you look faraway.
I find I am too slow

To catch your mood. I hear
The slow and far-off sea
And waves that beat a shore

That could be trying to
Call us toward our end,
make us hurry through

This little space of dark.
Yet love can stretch it wide.
Each life means so much work

You are my wealth, my pride.
The good side of me, see
That you stay by my side

Two roots of one great tree.

Friendship

ELIZABETH JENNINGS
(British; 1926–2001)

Such love I cannot analyse;
It does not rest in lips or eyes,
Neither in kisses nor caress.
Partly, I know, it's gentleness

And understanding in one word
Or in brief letters. It's preserved
By trust and by respect and awe.
These are the words I'm feeling for.

Two people, yes, two lasting friends.
The giving comes, the taking ends
There is no measure for such things.
For this all Nature slows and sings.

When, With You Asleep

JUAN RAMON JIMÉNEZ
(Spanish; 1881–1958)

When, with you asleep, I plunge into your soul,
and I listen, with my ear
on your naked breast,
to your tranquil heart, it seems to me
that, in its deep throbbing, I surprise

the secret of the center
of the world.

        It seems to me
that legions of angels
on celestial steeds
– as when, in the height
of the night we listen, without a breath
and our ears to the earth,
to distant hoofbeats that never arrive –,
that legions of angels are coming through you, from afar
– like the Three Kings
to the eternal birth
of our love –,
they are coming through you, from afar,
to bring me, in your dreams
the secret of the center
of the heavens.

Translated from the Spanish by Perry Higman.

To Celia

BEN JONSON
(English; 1573–1637)

Drink to me, only with thine eyes,
      And I will pledge with mine;
Or leave a kiss but in the cup,
      And I'll not look for wine.
The thirst, that from the soul doth rise,

Doth ask a drink divine:
But might I of Jove's nectar sup,
I would not change for thine.

I sent thee, late, a rosy wreath,
Not so much honouring thee,
As giving it a hope, that there
It could not withered be.
But thou thereon did'st only breathe,
And sent'st it back to me:
Since when it grows, and smells, I swear,
Not of itself, but thee.

The Sun Has Burst the Sky

JENNY JOSEPH
(British; 1932–   )

The sun has burst the sky
Because I love you
And the river its banks.

The sea laps the great rocks
Because I love you
And takes no heed of the moon dragging it away
And saying coldly 'Constancy is not for you'.

The blackbird fills the air
Because I love you
With spring and lawns and shadows falling on lawns.

The people walk in the street and laugh
I love you
And far down the river ships sound their hooters
Crazy with joy because I love you.

Married Love

KUAN TAO-SHENG
(Chinese; 1262–1319)

You and I
Have so much love
That it
Burns like a fire,
In which we bake a lump of clay
Molded into a figure of you
And a figure of me.
Then we take both of them,
And break them into pieces,
And mix the pieces with water,
And mold again a figure of you,
And a figure of me.
I am in your clay.
You are in my clay.
In life we share a single quilt.
In death we will share one bed.

Translated from the Chinese by Kenneth Rexroth and Ling Chung.

I Want To Breathe

JAMES LAUGHLIN
(American; 1914–97)

I want to breathe

you in I'm not talking about
perfume or even the sweet o-

dour of your skin but of the
air itself I want to share

your air inhaling what you
exhale I'd like to be that

close two of us breathing
each other as one as that

Kissing

DORIANNE LAUX
(American; 1952–   )

They are kissing, on a park bench,
on the edge of an old bed, in a doorway
or on the floor of a church. Kissing
as the streets fill with balloons
or soldiers, locusts or confetti, water
or fire or dust. Kissing down through
the centuries under the sun or stars, a dead tree,

an umbrella, amid derelicts. Kissing
as Christ carries his cross, as Gandhi
sings his speeches, as a bullet
careens through the air towards a child's
good heart. They are kissing,
long, deep, spacious kisses, exploring
the silence of the tongue, the mute
rungs of the upper palate, hungry
for the living flesh. They are still
kissing when the cars crash and the bombs
drop, when the babies are born crying
into the white air, when Mozart bends
to his bowl of soup and Stalin
bends to his garden. They are kissing
to begin the world again. Nothing
can stop them. They kiss until their lips
swell, their thick tongues quickening
to the budded touch, licking up
the sweet juices. I want to believe
they are kissing to save the world,
but they're not. All they know
is this press and need, these two-legged
beasts, their faces like roses crushed
together and opening, they are covering
their teeth, they are doing what they have to do
to survive the worst, they are sealing
the hard words in, they are dying
for our sins. In a broken world they are
practicing this simple and singular act
to perfection. They are holding
onto each other. They are kissing.

Divine Love

WILLIAM LAW
(British; 1686–1761)

Love is the Christ of God. Wherever it comes, it comes as the blessing and happiness of every natural life, as the restorer of every lost perfection, a redeemer from all evil, a fulfiller of all righteousness, and a peace of God which passeth all understanding.

Through all the universe of things nothing is uneasy, unsatisfied or restless but because it is not governed by love, or because its nature has not reached or attained the full birth of the spirit of love. For when that is done every hunger is satisfied, and all complaining, murmuring, accusing, resenting, revenging and striving are as totally suppressed and overcome as the coldness, thickness and horror of darkness are suppressed and overcome by the less breaking forth of the light.

If you ask why the spirit of love cannot be displeased, cannot be disappointed, cannot complain, accuse, resent or murmur, it is because divine love desires nothing but itself, it is its own good, it has all when it has itself, because nothing is good but itself and its own working; for love is God and he that dwelleth in God dwelleth in love.

From *The Spirit of Love.*

The Clue to Human Life

D. H. LAWRENCE
(British; 1885–1930)

Marriage is the clue to human life, but there is no marriage apart from the wheeling sun and the nodding earth, from the straying of the planets and the magnificence of the fixed stars. Is not a man different, utterly different, at dawn from what he is at sunset? and a woman too? And does not the changing harmony and discord of their variation make the secret music of life?

And is it not so throughout life? A man is different at thirty, at forty, at fifty, at sixty, at seventy: and the woman at his side is different. But is there not some strange conjunction in their differences? Is there not some peculiar harmony, through youth, the period of child-birth, the period of florescence and young children, the period of the woman's change of life, painful yet also a renewal, the period of waning passion but mellowing delight of affection, the dim, unequal period of the approach of death, when the man and woman look at one another with the dim apprehension of separation that is not really a separation: is there not, throughout it all, some unseen, unknown interplay of balance, harmony, completion, like some soundless symphony, which moves with a rhythm from phase to phase, so different, so very different in the various movements, and yet one symphony, made out of the soundless singing of two strange and incompatible lives, a man's and a woman's?

This is marriage, the mystery of marriage, marriage which fulfils itself here, in this life. We may well believe that in heaven there is no marrying or giving in marriage. All this has to be fulfilled here, and if it is not fulfilled here, it will never be fulfilled.

From *A Propos of Lady Chatterley's Lover.*

A Wedding Speech

D. H. LAWRENCE
(British; 1885–1930)

In the cottage big fires were burning, there were dozens of glasses on the table, and holly and mistletoe hanging up. The wedding party crowded in, and Tom Brangwen, becoming roisterous, poured out drinks. Everybody must drink. The bells were ringing away against the windows.

'Lift your glasses up,' shouted Tom Brangwen from the parlour, 'lift your glasses up, an' drink to the hearth an' home – hearth an' home, an' may they enjoy it.'

'Night an' day, an' may they enjoy it,' shouted Frank Brangwen, in addition.

'Hammer an' tongs, and may they enjoy it,' shouted Alfred Brangwen, the saturnine…

Tom Brangwen wanted to make a speech. For the first time in his life, he must spread himself wordily.

'Marriage,' he began, his eyes twinkling and yet quite profound, for he was deeply serious and hugely amused at the same time, 'Marriage,' he said…is what we're made for –'

'Let him talk,' said Alfred Brangwen, slowly and inscrutably, 'let him talk.' Mrs Alfred darted indignant eyes at her husband.

'A man,' continued Tom Brangwen, 'enjoys being a man: for what purpose was he made a man, if not to enjoy it?'

'That a true word,' said Frank, floridly.

'And likewise,' continued Tom Brangwen, 'a woman enjoys being a woman: at least we surmise she does –'

'Oh don't you bother –' called a farmer's wife…

'Now,' continued Tom Brangwen, 'for a man to be a man, it takes a woman –'

'It does that,' said a woman grimly.

'And for a woman to be a woman, it takes a man –' continued Tom Brangwen.

'All speak up, men,' chimed in a feminine voice.

'Therefore we have marriage,' continued Tom Brangwen.

'Hold, hold,' said Alfred Brangwen. 'Don't run us off our legs.'

And in dead silence the glasses were filled. The bride and bridegroom, two children, sat with intent, shining faces at the head of the table, abstracted.

'There's no marriage in heaven,' went on Tom Brangwen; 'but on earth there is marriage.'

'That's the difference between 'em,' said Alfred Brangwen, mocking.

'Alfred,' said Tom Brangwen, 'keep your remarks till afterwards, and then we'll thank you for them. – There's very little else, on earth, but marriage. You can talk about making money, or saving souls. You can save your own soul seven times over, and you may have a mint of money, but your soul goes gnawin', gnawin', gnawin', and it says there's something it must have. In heaven there is no marriage. But on earth there is marriage, else heaven drops out and there's no bottom to it.'

'Just hark you now,' said Frank's wife.

'Go on, Thomas,' said Alfred sardonically.

'If we've got to be Angels,' went on Tom Brangwen, haranguing the company at large, 'and if there is no such thing as a man nor a woman amongst them, then it seems to me as a married couple makes one Angel.'

'It's the brandy,' said Alfred Brangwen wearily . . .

And a laugh went round the table. But Tom Brangwen was inspired.

'An Angel's got to be more than a human being,' he continued. 'So I say, an Angel is the soul of man and woman in one: they rise united at the Judgement Day, as one Angel –'

'Praising the Lord,' said Frank.

'Praising the Lord,' repeated Tom.

From *The Rainbow*.

The Long, Marital Embrace

D. H. LAWRENCE
(British; 1885–1930)

Was his life nothing? Had he nothing to show, no work? He did not count his work, anybody could have done it. What had he known, but the long, marital embrace with his wife! Curious, that this was what his life amounted to! At any rate, it was something, it was eternal. He would say so to anybody, and be proud of it. He lay with his wife in his arms, and she was still his fulfilment, just the same as ever. And that was the be-all and the end-all. Yes, and he was proud of it.

From *The Rainbow*.

The Owl and the Pussy Cat

EDWARD LEAR
(British; 1812–88)

The Owl and the Pussy-Cat went to sea
    In a beautiful pea-green boat.
They took some honey, and plenty of money
    Wrapped up in a five-pound note.
The Owl looked up to the stars above,
    And sang to a small guitar,

'O lovely Pussy! O Pussy, my love,
What a beautiful Pussy you are,
       You are,
       You are!
What a beautiful Pussy you are!'

Pussy said to the Owl, 'You elegant fowl!
  How charmingly sweet you sing!
O let us be married! too long we have tarried:
  But what shall we do for a ring?'
They sailed away, for a year and a day,
  To the land where the Bong-Tree grows,
And there in a wood a Piggy-wig stood,
With a ring at the end of his nose,
       His nose,
       His nose!
With a ring at the end of his nose.

'Dear Pig, are you willing to sell for one shilling
  Your ring?' Said the Piggy, 'I will.'
So they took it away, and were married next day
  By the turkey who lives on the hill.
They dined on mince, and slices of quince,
  Which they ate with a runcible spoon;
And hand in hand, on the edge of the sand
They danced by the light of the moon,
       The moon,
       The moon,
They danced by the light of the moon.

On 'Being in Love'

C. S. LEWIS
(British; 1898–1963)

People get from books the idea that if you have married the right person you may expect to go on 'being in love' for ever. As a result, when they find they are not, they think this proves they have made a mistake and are entitled to a change – not realising that, when they have changed, the glamour will presently go out of the new love just as it went out of the old one. In this department of life, as in every other, thrills come at the beginning and do not last.

Let the thrill go – let it die away – go on through that period of death into the quieter interest and happiness that follow – and you will find you are living in a world of new thrills all the time. But if you decide to make thrills your regular diet and try to prolong them artificially, they will all get weaker and weaker, and fewer and fewer, and you will be a bored, disillusioned old man for the rest of your life. It is because so few people understand this that you find many middle-aged men and women maundering about their lost youth, at the very age when new horizons ought to be appearing and new doors opening all round them. It is much better fun to learn to swim than to go on endlessly (and hopelessly) trying to get back the feeling you had when you first went paddling as a small boy.

From *Mere Christianity*.

A Pattern Like a Dance

ANNE MORROW LINDBERGH
(American; 1906–2001)

A good relationship has a pattern like a dance and is built on some of the same rules. The partners do not need to hold on tightly, because they move confidently in the same pattern, intricate but gay and swift and free, like a country dance of Mozart's. To touch heavily would be to arrest the pattern, to check the endlessly changing beauty of its unfolding…The joy of such a pattern is not only the joy of creation or the joy of participation, it is also the joy of living in the moment. Lightness of touch and living in the moment are intertwined…

When each partner loves so completely that he has forgotten to ask himself whether or not he is loved in return; when he only knows that he loves and is moving to its music – then, and then only, are two people able to dance perfectly in tune to the same rhythm. Then, the pattern of the dance will support and rejoice in the natural swinging of our lives between sharing and solitude; between the intimate and the abstract; between the near and the far.

The pattern must reflect the changing tides of our lives and our emotions. When you love someone, you do not love them all the time, in exactly the same way, from moment to moment. We should not insist on this type of permanency and duration. The only continuity possible, in life as in love, is in growth, in fluidity – in freedom, in the sense that the dancers are free, barely touching as they pass, but partners in the same pattern.

From *Gift from the Sea*.

Poem

CHRISTOPHER LOGUE
(British; 1926–   )

If the night flights keep you awake
I will call London Airport and tell them
to land their dangerous junk elsewhere.

And if you fall asleep with the sleeve
of my jacket under your head,
sooner than wake you, I'll cut it off.

But if you say:
'Fix me a plug on this mixer',
I grumble and take my time.

Decade

AMY LOWELL
(American; 1874–1925)

When you came, you were like red wine and honey,
And the taste of you burnt my mouth with its sweetness.
Now you are like morning bread,
Smooth and pleasant.
I hardly taste you at all for I know your savour,
But I am completely nourished.

Sure Proof

NORMAN MacCAIG
(Scottish; 1910–96)

I can no more describe you
than I can put a thing for the first time
where it already is.

If I could make a ladder of light
or comb the hair of a dream girl with a real comb
or pour a table into a jug…

I'm not good at impossible things.
And that is why I'm sure
I will love you for my ever.

True Ways of Knowing

NORMAN MacCAIG
(Scottish; 1910–96)

Not an ounce excessive, not an inch too little,
Our easy reciprocations. You let me know
The way a boat would feel, if it could feel,
The intimate support of water.

The news you bring me has been news forever,
So that I understand what a stone would say
If only a stone could speak. Is it sad a grassblade
Can't know how it is lovely?

It is said that you can't know, except by hearsay
(My gossiping failing words) that you are the way
A water is that can clench its palm and crumple
A boat's confiding timbers?

But that's excessive, and too little. Knowing
The way a circle would describe its roundness,
We touch two selves and feel, complete and gentle,
The intimate support of being.

The way that flight would feel a bird flying
(If it could feel) is the way a space that's in
A stone that's in a water would know itself
If it had our way of knowing.

The Passionate Shepherd to His Love

CHRISTOPHER MARLOWE
(English; 1564–93)

Come live with me and be my love,
And we will all the pleasures prove,
That hills and valleys, dales and fields,
And all the craggy mountains yields.

There we will sit upon the rocks,
And see the shepherds feed their flocks,
By shallow rivers to whose falls
Melodious birds sing madrigals.

And I will make thee beds of roses
With a thousand fragrant posies,
A cap of flowers, and a kirtle
Embroidered all with leaves of myrtle;

A gown made of the finest wool
Which from our pretty lambs we pull;
Fair linèd slippers for the cold,
With buckles of the purest gold;

A belt of straw and ivy buds,
With coral clasps and amber studs:
And if these pleasures may thee move,
Come live with me and be my love.

The shepherds' swains shall dance and sing
For thy delight each May morning:
If these delights thy mind may move,
Then live with me and be my love.

Being Her Friend

JOHN MASEFIELD
(British; 1878–1967)

Being her friend, I do not care, not I,
How gods or men may wrong me, beat me down;
Her word's sufficient star to travel by,
I count her quiet praise sufficient crown.

Being her friend, I do not covet gold,
Save for a royal gift to give her pleasure;
To sit with her, and have her hand to hold,
Is wealth, I think, surpassing minted treasure.

Being her friend, I only covet art,
A white pure flame to search me as I trace
In crooked letters from a throbbing heart
The hymn to beauty written on her face.

The Bonds of Our Love

MATTHEW OF RIEVAULX
(English; c. 1109–1167)

The winter will lose its cold,
as the snow will be without whiteness,

The night without darkness,
the heavens without stars,

The day without light,

The flower will lose its beauty,
all fountains their water, the sea its fish,

The tree its birds, the forest its beasts,
the earth its harvest –

All these will pass before anyone breaks
the bonds of our love,
and before I cease caring for you
in my heart.

May your days be happy in number
as flakes of snow,
May your nights be peaceful
and may you be without troubles.

Translated from the Latin.

The First Marriage

PETER MEINKE
(American; 1932–   )

imagine the very first marriage a girl
and boy trembling with some inchoate
need for ceremony a desire for witness:
inventing formality like a wheel or a hoe

in a lost language in a clearing too far from here
a prophet or a prophetess intoned to the lovers
who knelt with their hearts cresting
like the unnamed ocean thinking *This is true*

thinking they will never be alone again
though planets slip their tracks and fish
desert the sea repeating those magic sounds
meaning *I do* on this stone below
this tree before these friends *yes* in body
and word my darkdream my sunsong yes *I do I do*

I Forget All Time

JOHN MILTON
(English; 1608–74)

With thee conversing, I forget all time,
All seasons, and their change, all please alike.
Sweet is the breath of morn, her rising sweet,
With charm of earliest birds; pleasant the sun,
When first on this delightful land he spreads
His orient beams, on herb, tree, fruit, and flower,
Glistening with dew; fragrant the fertile earth
After soft showers; and sweet the coming on
Of grateful evening mild, then silent night
With this her solemn bird, and this fair moon
And these the gems of heaven, her starry train:
But neither breath of morn, when she ascends
With charm of earliest birds, nor rising sun
On this delightful land, nor herb, fruit, flower,
Glistering with dew, nor fragrance after showers,
Nor grateful evening mild, nor silent night
With this her solemn bird, nor walk by moon
Or glittering starlight, without thee is sweet.

From *Paradise Lost*.

The Confirmation

EDWIN MUIR
(Scottish; 1887–1959)

Yes, yours, my love, is the right human face.
I in my mind had waited for this long,
Seeing the false and searching for the true,
Then found you as a traveller finds a place
Of welcome suddenly amid the wrong
Valleys and rocks and twisting roads. But you,
What shall I call you? A fountain in a waste,
A well of water in a country dry,
Or anything that's honest and good, an eye
That makes the whole world bright. Your open heart,
Simple with giving, gives the primal deed,
The first good world, the blossom, the blowing seed,
The hearth, the steadfast land, the wandering sea.
Not beautiful or rare in every part.
But like yourself, as they were meant to be.

Song

EDWIN MUIR
(Scottish; 1887–1959)

Why should your face so please me
That if one little line should stray
Bewilderment would seize me
And drag me down the tortuous way

Out of the noon into the night?
But so, into this tranquil light
You raise me.

How could our minds so marry
That, separate, blunder to and fro,
Make for a point, miscarry,
And blind as headstrong horses go?
Though now they in their promised land
At pleasure travel hand in hand
Or tarry.

This concord is an answer
To questions far beyond our mind
Whose image is a dancer.
All effort is to ease refined
Here, weight is light; this is the dove
Of love and peace, not heartless love
The lancer.

And yet I still must wonder
That such an armistice can be
And life roll by in thunder
To leave this calm with you and me.
This tranquil voice of silence, yes,
This single song of two, this is
A wonder.

The Strange Case of Mr Ormantude's Bride

OGDEN NASH

(American; 1902–71)

Once there was a bridegroom named Mr Ormantude whose
    intentions were hard to disparage,
Because he intended to make his a happy marriage,
And he succeeded for going on fifty years,
During which he was in marital bliss up to his ears.
His wife's days and nights were enjoyable
Because he catered to every foible;
He went around humming hymns
And anticipating her whims.
Many a fine bit of repartee died on his lips
Lest it throw her anecdotes into eclipse;
He was always silent when his cause was meritorious,
And he never engaged in argument unless sure he was so
    obviously wrong that she couldn't help emerging victorious,
And always when in her vicinity
He was careful to make allowances for her femininity;
Were she snappish, he was sweetish,
And of understanding her he made a fetish.
Everybody said his chances of celebrating his golden wedding
    looked good,
But on his golden wedding eve he was competently poisoned by
    his wife who could no longer stand being perpetually
    understood.

I Do, I Will, I Have

OGDEN NASH
(American; 1902–71)

How wise I am to have instructed the butler to instruct the first
   footman to instruct the second footman to instruct the
   doorman to order my carriage;
I am about to volunteer a definition of marriage.
Just as I know that there are two Hagens, Walter and Copen,
I know that marriage is a legal and religious alliance entered
   into by a man who can't sleep with the window shut and a
   woman who can't sleep with the window open.
Moreover, just as I am unsure of the difference between flora
   and fauna and flotsam and jetsam,
I am quite sure that marriage is the alliance of two eople one of
   whom never remembers birthdays and the other never
   forgetsam,
And he refuses to believe there is a leak in the water pipe or the
   gas pipe and she is convinced she is about to asphyxiate or
   drown,
And she says Quick get up and get my hairbrushes off the
   windowsill, it's raining in, and he replies Oh they're all right,
   it's only raining straight down.
That is why marriage is so much more interesting than divorce,
Because it's the only known example of the happy meeting of
   the immovable object and the irresistible force.
So I hope husbands and wives will continue to debate and
   combat over everything debatable and combatable,
Because I believe a little incompatibility is the spice of life,
   particularly if he has income and she is pattable.

In September

JOHN ORMOND
(Welsh; 1923–90)

Again the golden month, still
Favourite, is renewed;
Once more I'd wind it in a ring
About your finger, pledge myself
Again, my love, my shelter,
My good roof over me,
My strong wall against winter.

Be bread upon my table still
And red wine in my glass; be fire
Upon my hearth. Continue,
My true storm door, continue
To be sweet lock to my key;
Be wife to me, remain
The soft silk on my bed.

Be morning to my pillow,
Multiply my joy. Be my rare coin
For counting, my luck, my
Granary, my promising fair
Sky, my star, the meaning
Of my journey. Be, this year too,
My twelve months long desire.

Wedding

ALICE OSWALD
(British; 1966–   )

From time to time our love is like a sail
and when the sail begins to alternate
from tack to tack, it's like a swallowtail
and when the swallow flies it's like a coat;
and if the coat is yours, it has a tear
like a wide mouth and when the mouth begins
to draw the wind, it's like a trumpeter
and when the trumpet blows, it blows like millions
and this, my love, when millions come and go
beyond the need of us, is like a trick;
and when the trick begins, it's like a toe
tiptoeing on a rope, which is like luck;
and when the luck begins, it's like a wedding,
which is like love, which is like everything.

It Takes Years To Marry Completely

THEODORE PARKER
(American; 1810–60)

It takes years to marry completely two hearts, even of the most loving and well assorted. A happy wedlock is a long falling in love. Young persons think love belongs only to the brown-haired and crimson-cheeked. So it does for its beginning. But the golden marriage is a part of love which the bridal day knows nothing of...

Such a large and sweet fruit is a complete marriage that it needs a long summer to ripen in, and then a long winter to mellow and season it. But a really happy marriage of love and judgment between a noble man and woman is one of the things so very handsome that if the sun were, as the Greeks once fabled, a God he might stop the world and hold it still now and then in order to look all day long on some example thereof, and feast his eyes on such a spectacle.

Her Song

BRIAN PATTEN
(British; 1946–   )

For no other reason than I love him wholly
I am here; for this one night at least
The world has shrunk to a boyish breast
On which my head, brilliant and exhausted, rests,
And can know of nothing more complete.

Let the dawn assemble all its guilts, its worries
And small doubts that, but for love, would infect
This perfect heart.
I am as far beyond doubt as the sun.
I am as far beyond doubt as is possible.

When You Wake Tomorrow

BRIAN PATTEN
(British; 1946–   )

I will give you a poem when you wake tomorrow.
It will be a peaceful poem.
It won't make you sad.
It won't make you miserable.
It will simply be a poem to give you
when you wake tomorrow.

It was not written by myself alone.
I cannot lay claim to it.
I found it in your body.
In your smile I found it.
Will you recognise it?

You will find it under your pillow.
When you open the cupboard it will be there.
You will blink in astonishment,
shout out, 'How it trembles!
Its nakedness is startling! How fresh it tastes!'

We will have it for breakfast;
on a table lit by loving,
at a place reserved for wonder.
We will give the world a kissing open
when we wake tomorrow.

We will offer it to the sad landlord out on the balcony.
To the dreamers at the window.
To the hand waving for no particular reason
we will offer it.
An amazing and most remarkable thing,
we will offer it to the whole human race
which walks in us
when we wake tomorrow.

Right Marriage

WILLIAM PENN
(English; 1644–1718)

Never marry but for love; but see that thou lov'st what is lovely. If love be not thy chiefest motive, thou wilt soon grow weary of a married state and stray from thy promise, to search out thy pleasures in forbidden places…

But in marriage do thou be wise; prefer the person before money, virtue before beauty, the mind before the body. Then hast thou a wife, a friend, a companion, a second self, one that bears an equal joy with thee in all thy toils and troubles.

Choose one that measures her satisfaction, safety and danger, by thine; and of whom thou art sure, as of thy secretest thoughts: a friend as well as a wife, which indeed a wife implies: for she is but half a wife that is not, or is not capable of being such a friend…

Nothing can be more entire and without reserve; nothing more zealous, affectionate and sincere; nothing more contented and constant than such a couple; nor no greater temporal felicity than to be one of them.

Between a man and his wife nothing ought to rule but love…As love ought to bring them together, so it is the best way to keep them well together.

From *Fruits of Solitude.*

In Praise of Love

PLATO
(Greek; 429–347 BC)

Therefore…I say of Love that he is the fairest and best in himself, and the cause of what is fairest and best in all other things…This is he who empties men of disaffection and fills them with affection, who makes them to meet together at banquets such as these: in sacrifices, feasts, dances, he is our lord – who sends courtesy and sends away discourtesy, who gives kindness ever and never gives unkindness; the friend of the good, the wonder of the wise, the amazement of the gods; desired by those who have no part in him, and precious to those who have the better part in him; parent of delicacy, luxury, desire, fondness, softness, grace; regardful of the good, regardless of the evil: in every word, work, wish, fear – saviour, pilot, comrade, helper; glory of gods and men, leader best and brightest: in whose footsteps let every man follow, sweetly singing in his honour and joining in that sweet strain with which love charms the souls of gods and men.

From *The Symposium*; translated from the Greek by Benjamin Jowett.

My Beloved Is Mine and I Am His: He Feedeth Among the Lillies

FRANCIS QUARLES
(English; 1592–1644)

Even like two little bank-dividing brooks,
  That wash the pebbles with their wanton streams,
And having ranged and searched a thousand nooks,
  Meet both at length in silver-breasted Thames
    Where in a greater current they conjoin:
So I my Best-Beloved's am, so he is mine.

Even so we met; and after long pursuit
  Even so we joined; we both became entire;
No need for either to renew a suit,
  For I was flax and he was flames of fire:
    Our firm united souls did more than twine,
So I my Best-Beloved's am, so he is mine.

If all those glittering monarchs that command
  The servile quarters of this earthly ball
Should tender in exchange their shares of land,
  I would not change my fortunes for them all:
    Their wealth is but a counter to my coin;
The world's but theirs, but my Beloved's mine.

Nor time, nor place, nor chance, nor death can bow
  My least desires unto the least remove;
He's firmly mine by oath, I his by vow;
  He's mine by faith, and I am his by love;
    He's mine by water, I am his by wine;
Thus I my Best-Beloved's am, thus he is mine

...

He is my altar, I his holy place;
  I am his guest, and he my living food;
I'm his by penitence, he mine by grace;
  I'm his by purchase, he is mine by blood;
    He's my supporting elm, and I his vine;
Thus I my Best-Beloved's am, thus he is mine.

He gives me wealth, I give him all my vows;
  I give him songs, he gives me length of days;
With wreaths of grace he crowns my conquering brows;
  And I his temples with a crown of praise,
    Which he accepts as an everlasting sign,
That I my Best-Beloved's am; that he is mine.

Amo Ergo Sum

KATHLEEN RAINE
(British; 1908–2003)

Because I love
  The sun pours out its rays of living gold
  Pours out its gold and silver on the sea.

Because I love
  The earth upon her astral spindle winds
  Her ecstasy-producing dance.

Because I love
  Clouds travel on the winds through wide skies,
  Skies wide and beautiful, blue and deep.

Because I love
  Wind blows white sails,
  The wind blows over flowers, the sweet wind blows.

Because I love
  The ferns grown green, and green the grass, and green
  The transparent sunlit trees.

Because I love
  Larks rise up from the grass
  And all the leaves are full of singing birds.

Because I love
  The summer air quivers with a thousand wings,
  Myriads of jewelled eyes burn in the light.

Because I love
  The iridescent shells upon the sand
  Take forms as fine and intricate as thought.

Because I love
  There is an invisible way across the sky,
  Birds travel by that way, the sun and moon
  And all the stars travel that path by night.

Because I love
  There is a river flowing all night long.

Because I love
  All night the river flows into my sleep,
  Ten thousand living things are sleeping in my arms,
  And sleeping wake, and flowing are at rest.

A Marvellous Living Side by Side

RAINER MARIA RILKE
(Austrian; 1875–1926)

Marriage is in many ways a simplification of life. It naturally combines the strengths and wills of two young people so that, together, they seem to reach farther into the future than they did before. Above all, marriage is a new task and a new seriousness, a new demand on the strength and generosity of each partner.

The point of marriage is not to create a quick commonality by tearing down all boundaries; on the contrary, a good marriage is one in which each partner appoints the other to be the guardian of their solitude, and thus they show each other the greatest possible trust. A merging of two people is an impossibility, but once the realization is accepted that even between the closest people infinite distances exist, a marvellous living side by side can grow up for them, if they succeed in loving the expanse between them, which gives them the possibility of always seeing each other as a whole and before an immense sky.

From *Letters to a Young Poet*; translated from the German by Stephen Mitchell.

To Love Another

RAINER MARIA RILKE
(Austrian; 1875–1926)

For one human being to love another human being: that is perhaps the most difficult task that has been entrusted to us, the ultimate task, the final test and proof, the work for which all other work is merely preparation. That is why young people, who are beginners in everything, are not yet capable of love: it is something they must learn. With their whole being, with all their forces, gathered around their solitary, anxious, upward-beating heart, they must learn to love. But learning-time is always a long, secluded time…Loving does not at first mean merging, surrendering, and uniting with another person (for what would a union be of two people who are unclarified, unfinished, and still incoherent?), it is a high inducement for the individual to ripen, to become something in himself, to become world, to become world in himself for the sake of another person; it is a great, demanding claim on him, something that chooses him and calls him to vast distances.

From *Letters to a Young Poet*; translated from the German by Stephen Mitchell.

A Birthday

CHRISTINA ROSSETTI
(British; 1830–94)

My heart is like a singing bird
    Whose nest is in a watered shoot;
My heart is like an apple tree
    Whose boughs are bent with thickset fruit;
My heart is like a rainbow shell
    That paddles in a halcyon sea;
My heart is gladder than all of these
    Because my love is come to me.

Raise me a dais of silk and down;
    Hang it with vair and purple dyes;
Carve it in doves and pomegranates
    And peacocks with a hundred eyes;
Work it in gold and silver grapes,
    In leaves and silver fleurs-de-lys;
Because the birthday of my life
    Is come, my love is come to me.

That First Day

CHRISTINA ROSSETTI
(British; 1830–94)

I wish I could remember, that first day,
    First hour, first moment of your meeting me,

If bright or dim the season, it might be
Summer or Winter for aught I can say;
So unrecorded did it slip away,
  So blind was I to see and to foresee,
  So dull to mark the budding of my tree
That would not blossom yet for many a May.
If only I could recollect it, such
  A day of days! I let it come and go
  As traceless as a thaw of bygone snow;
It seemed to mean so little, meant so much;
If only now I could recall that touch,
First touch of hand in hand – Did one but know!

Sudden Light

DANTE GABRIEL ROSSETTI
(British; 1828–82)

I have been here before,
But when or how I cannot tell:
I know the grass beyond the door,
The sweet keen smell,
The sighing sound, the lights around the shore.

You have been mine before –
How long ago I may not know:
But just when at that swallow's soar
Your neck turned so,
Some veil did fall – I knew it all or yore.

Has this been thus before?
And shall not thus time's eddying flight
Still with our lives our love restore
In death's despite,
And day and night yield one delight once more?

Quatrain

JALAL AL-DIN RUMI
(Persian; 1207–73)

The minute I heard my first love story
I started looking for you, not knowing
    how blind that was.

Lovers don't finally meet somewhere,
they're in each other all along.

Translated from the Persian by Coleman Barks.

The Taste of Morning

JALAL AL-DIN RUMI
(Persian; 1207–73)

Time's knife slides from the sheath,
as a fish from where it swims.

Being closer and closer is the desire
of the body. Don't wish for union!

There's a closeness beyond that. Why
would God want a second God? Fall in

love in such a way that it frees you
from any connecting. Love is the soul's

light, the taste of morning, no me, no
we, no claim of being. These words

are the smoke the fire gives off as it
absolves its defects, as eyes in silence,

tears, face. Love cannot be said.

Translated from the Persian by Coleman Barks.

Passionate Mutual Love

BERTRAND RUSSELL
(British; 1872–1970)

Love is something far more than desire for sexual intercourse; it is the principle means of escape from the loneliness which affects most men and women throughout the greater part of their lives. There is a deep-seated fear, in most people, of the cold world and the possible cruelty of the herd; there is a longing for affection, which is often concealed by roughness, boorishness or a bullying manner in men, and by nagging and scolding in women. Passionate mutual love while it lasts puts an end to this feeling; it breaks down the hard walls of the ego, producing a new being composed of two in one. Nature did not construct human beings to stand alone, since they cannot fulfil her biological purpose except with the help of another; and civilized people cannot fully satisfy their sexual instinct without love. The instinct is not completely satisfied unless a man's whole being, mental quite as much as physical, enters into the relation. Those who have never known the deep intimacy and the intense companionship of mutual love have missed the best thing that life has to give…if they miss this experience, men and women cannot attain their full stature, and cannot feel towards the rest of the world that kind of generous warmth without which their social activities are pretty sure to be harmful.

From *Marriage and Morals.*

A Love Song

VERNON SCANNELL
(British; 1922–   )

I've always been in love with you I swear
'Impossible,' they say, yet it is true:
I speak with certainty, for I was there.

When I reeled groggy as the punchbowl air
Was spiced with melody I longed for you;
I've always been in love with you I swear.

My infant whispers to the beat-up bear
Were meant for you, the tears and kisses too;
I speak with certainty, for I was there.

Let experts, calendars and maps declare
I'm nuts or have at least one wobbly screw;
I've always been in love with you I swear.

New kinds of beauty and the wish to share
These riches were rehearsals, as I knew;
I speak with certainty, for I was there.

These shadow-loves were work-outs to prepare
For this, the main event, that they led to;
I've always been in love with you I swear;
I speak with certainty, for I was there.

A Secret to Each Other

ALBERT SCHWEITZER
(German; 1875–1965)

We are each a secret to the other. To know one another cannot mean to know everything about each other; it means to feel mutual affection and confidence, and to believe in one another. We must not try to force our way into the personality of another. To analyse others is a rude commencement, for there is a modesty of the soul which we must recognise just as we do that of the body. No one has a right to say to another: 'Because we belong to each other as we do, I have a right to know all your thoughts.' Not even a mother may treat her child in that way. All demands of this sort are foolish and unwholesome. In this matter giving is the only valuable process; it is only giving that stimulates. Impart as much as you can of your spiritual being to those who are on the road with you, and accept as something precious what comes back to you from them.

From *Memories of Childhood and Youth*.

An Hour with Thee

SIR WALTER SCOTT
(Scottish; 1771–1832)

An hour with thee! When earliest day
Dapples with gold the eastern grey,
Oh, what can frame my mind to bear

The toil and turmoil, cark and care,
New griefs, which coming hours unfold,
And sad remembrance of the old?
    One hour with thee.

One hour with thee! When burning June
Waves his red flag at pitch of noon;
What shall repay the faithful swain,
His labour on the sultry plain;
And, more than cave or sheltering bough,
Cool feverish blood and throbbing brow?
    One hour with thee.

One hour with thee! When sun is set,
Oh, what can teach me to forget
The thankless labours of the day;
The hopes, the wishes, flung away;
The increasing wants, and lessening gains,
The master's pride, who scorns my pains?
    One hour with thee.

A Betrothal

E. J. SCOVELL
(British; 1907–99)

Put your hand on my heart, say that you love me as
The woods upon the hills cleave to the hills' contours.
I will uphold you, trunk and shoot and flowering sheaf,
And I will hold you, roots and fruit and fallen leaf.

To Cloris

SIR CHARLES SEDLEY
(English; ?1639–1701)

Cloris, I cannot say your eyes
Did my unwary heart surprise;
Nor will I swear it was your face,
Your shape, or any nameless grace:
For you are so entirely fair,
To love a part, injustice were;
No drowning man can know which drop
Of water his last breath did stop;
So when the stars in heaven appear,
And join to make the night look clear;
The light we no one's bounty call,
But the obliging gift of all.
He that does lips or hands adore,
Deserves them only, and no more;
But I love all, and every part,
And nothing less can ease my heart.
Cupid, that lover, weakly strikes,
Who can express what 'tis he likes.

Sonnet XVIII

WILLIAM SHAKESPEARE
(English; 1564–1616)

Shall I compare thee to a summer's day?
  Thou art more lovely and more temperate:
Rough winds do shake the darling buds of May,
  And summer's lease hath all too short a date;
Sometime too hot the eye of heaven shines,
  And often is his gold complexion dimmed;
And every fair from fair sometimes declines,
  By chance, or nature's changing course untrimmed;
But thy eternal summer shall not fade,
  Nor lose possession of that fair thou owest,
Nor shall Death brag thou wanderest in his shade,
  When in eternal lines to time thou growest;
    So long as men can breathe, or eyes can see,
    So long lives this, and this gives life to thee.

Sonnet CXVI

WILLIAM SHAKESPEARE
(English; 1564–1616)

Let me not to the marriage of true minds
  Admit impediments. Love is not love
Which alters when it alteration finds,
  Or bends with the remover to remove:

Oh no, it is an ever fixèd mark
    That looks on tempests and is never shaken;
It is the star to every wandering bark,
    Whose worth's unknown, although his height be taken.
Love's not Time's fool, though rosy lips and cheeks
    Within his bending sickle's compass come;
Love alters not with his brief hours and weeks,
    But bears it out even to the edge of doom.
        If this be error and upon me proved,
        I never writ, nor no man ever loved.

Love's Power

WILLIAM SHAKESPEARE
(English; 1564–1616)

But love, first learnèd in a lady's eyes,
Lives not alone immurèd in the brain,
But, with the motion of all elements,
Courses as swift as thought in every power,
And gives to every power a double power,
Above their functions and their offices.
It adds a precious seeing to the eye;
A lover's eyes will gaze an eagle blind;
A lover's ear will hear the lowest sound,
When the suspicious head of theft is stopped:
Love's feeling is more soft and sensible
Than are the tender horns of cockled snails:
Love's tongue proves dainty Bacchus gross in taste.
For valour, is not Love a Hercules

Still climbing trees in the Hesperides?
Subtle as Sphinx; as sweet and musical
As bright Apollo's lute, strung with his hair;
And when Love speaks, the voice of all the gods
Makes heaven drowsy with the harmony.
Never durst poet touch a pen to write
Until his ink were tempered with Love's sighs;
O! then his lines would ravish savage ears,
And plant in tyrants mild humility.
From women's eyes this doctrine I derive:
They sparkle still the right Promethean fire;
They are the books, the arts, the academes,
That show, contain, and nourish all the world;
Else none at all in aught proves excellent.

From *Love's Labour's Lost*.

Boundless Love

WILLIAM SHAKESPEARE
(English; 1564–1616)

My bounty is as boundless as the sea,
My love as deep; the more I give to thee,
The more I have, for both are infinite.

From *Romeo and Juliet*.

Florizel to Perdita

WILLIAM SHAKESPEARE
(English; 1564–1616)

What you do
Still betters what is done. When you speak, sweet,
I'd have you do it ever: when you sing,
I'd have you buy and sell so; so give alms;
Pray so; and, for the ordering your affairs,
To sing them too: when you do dance, I wish you
A wave o' the sea, that you might ever do
Nothing but that; move still, still so,
And own no other function: each your doing,
So singular in each particular,
Crowns what you are doing in the present deed,
That all your acts are queens.

From *The Winter's Tale.*

Bridal Song

WILLIAM SHAKESPEARE
(English; 1564–1616)

Roses, their sharp spines being gone,
Not royal in their smells alone,
    But in their hue;

Maiden pinks, of odour faint,
Daisies smell-less, yet most quaint,
   And sweet thyme true;

Primrose, firstborn child of Ver,
Merry springtime's harbinger,
   With her bells dim;
Oxlips in their cradles growing,
Marigolds on death-beds blowing,
   Larks'-heels trim:

All dear Nature's children sweet
Lie 'fore bride and bridegroom's feet,
   Blessing their sense.
Not an angel of the air,
Bird melodious or bird fair,
   Be absent hence.

The crow, the slanderous cuckoo, nor
The boding raven, nor chough hoar,
   Nor chattering pie,
May on our bride-house perch or sing,
Or with them any discord bring,
   But from it fly.

From *The Two Noble Kinsmen*; sometimes attributed to
John Fletcher (English; 1579–1625).

Love's Philosophy

PERCY BYSSHE SHELLEY
(British; 1792–1822)

The fountains mingle with the river
And the rivers with the ocean,
The winds of Heaven mix for ever
With a sweet emotion;
Nothing in the world is single;
All things by a law divine
In one spirit meet and mingle.
Why not I with thine? –

See the mountains kiss high Heaven
And the waves clasp one another;
No sister-flower would be forgiven
If it disdained its brother;
And the sunlight clasps the earth
And the moonbeams kiss the sea:
What is all this sweet work worth
If thou kiss not me?

What Is Love?

PERCY BYSSHE SHELLEY
(British; 1792–1822)

What is love? Ask him who lives, what is life? ask him who adores, what is God? It is that powerful attraction towards all that we conceive, or fear, or hope beyond ourselves, when we find within our own thoughts the chasm of an insufficient void, and seek to awaken in all things that are, a community with what we experience within ourselves. If we reason, we would be understood; if we imagine, we would that the airy children of our brain were born anew within another's; if we feel, we would that another's nerves should vibrate to our own, that the beams of their eyes should kindle at once and mix and melt into our own, that lips of motionless ice should not reply to lips quivering and burning with the heart's best blood. This is Love. This is the bond and the sanction which connects not only man with man, but with everything which exists.

From *On Love*.

My True Love Hath My Heart

SIR PHILIP SIDNEY
(English; 1554–86)

My true love hath my heart, and I have his,
  By just exchange, one for the other given.
I hold his dear, and mine he cannot miss,

There never was a better bargain driven.
His heart in me keeps me and him in one,
    My heart in him his thoughts and senses guides;
He loves my heart, for once it was his own,
    I cherish his, because in me it bides.
His heart his wound receivèd from my sight,
    My heart was wounded with his wounded heart;
For as from me on him his hurt did light,
    So still methought in me his hurt did smart.
      Both equal hurt, in this change sought our bliss:
    My true love hath my heart and I have his.

I Will Make You Brooches

ROBERT LOUIS STEVENSON
(Scottish; 1850–94)

I will make you brooches, and toys for your delight,
Of bird-song at morning and star-shine at night.
I will make a palace fit for you and me
Of green days in forests and blue days at sea.

I will make my kitchen, and you shall keep your room,
Where white flows the river and bright blows the broom,
And you shall wash your linen and keep your body white
In rainfall at morning and dewfall at night.

And this shall be for music when no one else is near,
The fine song for singing, the rare song to hear!
That only I remember, that only you admire,
Of the broad road that stretches and the roadside fire.

One Long Conversation

ROBERT LOUIS STEVENSON
(Scottish; 1850–94)

Marriage is one long conversation, chequered by disputes. The disputes are valueless; they but ingrain the difference; the heroic heart of woman prompting her at once to nail her colours to the mast. But in the intervals, almost unconsciously and with no desire to shine, the whole material of life is turned over and over, ideas are struck out and shared, the two persons more and more adapt their notions one to suit the other, and in process of time, without sound of trumpet, they conduct each other into new worlds of thought.

From *Memories and Portraits.*

True Love

WISŁAW SZYMBORSKA

(Polish; 1923–   )

True love. Is it normal
is it serious, is it practical?
What does the world get from two people
who exist in a world of their own?

Placed on the same pedestal for no good reason,
drawn randomly from millions but convinced
it had to happen this way – in reward for what?
For nothing.

The light descends from nowhere.
Why on these two and not on others?
Doesn't this outrage justice? Yes it does.
Doesn't it disrupt our painstakingly erected principles,
and cast the moral from the peak? Yes on both accounts.

Look at the happy couple.
Couldn't they at least try to hide it,
fake a little depression for their friends' sake?
Listen to them laughing – it's an insult.
The language they use – deceptively clear.
And their little celebrations, rituals,
the elaborate mutual routines –
it's obviously a plot behind the human race's back!

It's hard even to guess how far things might go
if people start to follow their example.
What could religion and poetry count on?
What would be remembered? What renounced?
Who'd want to stay within bounds?

True love. Is it really necessary?
Tact and common sense tell us to pass over it in silence,
like a scandal in Life's highest circles.
Perfectly good children are born without its help.
It couldn't populate the planet in a million years,
it comes along so rarely.

Let the people who never find true love
keep saying that there's no such thing.

Their faith will make it easier for them to live and die.

Translated from the Polish by Stanisław Barańczak and Clare Cavanagh.

Send Me the Love

RABINDRANATH TAGORE
(Indian; 1861–1941)

Not for me is the love that knows no restraint, but like the foaming
wine that having burst its vessel in a moment would run to waste.

Send me the love which is cool and pure like your rain that blesses the
thirsty earth and fills the homely earthen jars.

Send me the love that would soak down into the centre of being, and
from there would spread like the unseen sap through the branch-
ing tree of life, giving birth to fruits and flowers.

Send me the love that keeps the heart still with the fulness of peace.

From *Fruit Gathering*, translated from the Bengali by the author.

The State of Marriage

JEREMY TAYLOR
(English; 1613–67)

Marriage is a school and exercise of virtue; and though marriage hath
cares, yet the single life hath desires, which are more troublesome and
more dangerous…here is the proper scene of piety and patience, of
the duty of parents and the charity of relations; here kindness is spread
abroad, and love is united and made firm as a centre; marriage is the
nursery of Heaven…The state of marriage…hath in it the labour of
love, and the delicacies of friendship, the blessing of society, and the

union of hands and hearts. It hath in it less of beauty, but more of safety, than the single life…it is more merry, and more sad; is fuller of sorrows, and fuller of joys; it lies under more burdens, but it is supported by all the strengths of love and charity, and those burdens are delightful. Marriage is the mother of the world, and preserves kingdoms, and fills cities, and churches, and heaven itself. Celibacy, like the fly in the heart of an apple, dwells in a perpetual sweetness, but sits alone, and is confined and dies in singularity; but marriage, like the useful bee, builds a house, and gathers sweetness from every flower, and labours and unites into societies and republics…and keeps order, and exercises many virtues, and promotes the interest of mankind, and is the state of good things to which God hath designed the present constitution of the world.

From *The Marriage Ring; or the Mysteries and Duties of Marriage.*

I Would Live in Your Love

SARA TEASDALE
(American; 1884–1933)

I would live in your love as the sea-grasses live in the sea,
Borne up by each wave as it passes, drawn down by each wave
　　that recedes;
I would empty my soul of the dreams that have gathered in
　　me,
I would beat with your heart as it beats, I would follow your
　　soul as it leads.

Marriage Morning

ALFRED, LORD TENNYSON
(British; 1809–92)

Light, so low upon earth,
  You send a flash to the sun.
Here is the golden close of love,
  All my wooing is done.
Oh, the woods and the meadows,
  Wood where we hid from the wet,
Stiles where we stayed to be kind,
Meadows in which we met!

Light, so low in the vale
  You flash and lighten afar,
For this is the golden morning of love,
  And you are his morning star.
Flash, I am coming, I come,
  By meadow and stile and wood,
Oh, lighten into my eyes and heart,
  Into my heart and my blood!

Heart, are you great enough
  For a love that never tires?
O heart, are you great enough for love?
  I have heard of thorns and briers.
Over the thorns and briers,
  Over the meadows and stiles,
Over the world to the end of it
  Flash for a million miles.

Now Sleeps the Crimson Petal

ALFRED, LORD TENNYSON
(British; 1809–92)

Now sleeps the crimson petal, now the white;
Nor waves the cypress in the palace walk;
Nor winks the gold fin in the porphyry font:
The fire-fly wakens: waken thou with me.

Now droops the milkwhite peacock like a ghost,
And like a ghost she glimmers on to me.

Now lies the Earth all Danaë to the stars,
And all thy heart lies open unto me.

Now slides the silent meteor on, and leaves
A shining furrow, as thy thoughts in me.

Now folds the lily all her sweetness up,
And slips into the bosom of the lake:
So fold thyself, my dearest, thou, and slip
Into my bosom and be lost in me.

From *The Princess.*

Not Love Perhaps

A. S. J. TESSIMOND
(British; 1902–62)

This is not Love perhaps – Love that lays down
Its life, that many waters cannot quench, nor the floods
    drown –
But something written in lighter ink, said in a lower tone:
Something perhaps especially our own:
A need at times to be together and talk –
And then the finding we can walk
More firmly through dark narrow places
And meet more easily nightmare faces:
A need to reach out sometimes hand to hand –
And then find Earth less like an alien land:
A need for alliance to defeat
The whisperers at the corner of the street:
A need for inns on roads, islands in seas, halts for
    discoveries to be shared,
Maps checked and notes compared:
A need at times of each for each
Direct as the need of throat and tongue for speech.

Love Is a Great Thing

THOMAS À KEMPIS
(German: c. 1380–1471)

Love is a great thing, yea, a great and thorough good; by itself it makes that is heavy light, and it bears evenly all that is uneven.

It carries a burden which is no burden; it will not be kept back by anything low and mean; it desires to be free from all wordly affections, and not to be entangled by any outward prosperity, or by any adversity subdued.

Love feels no burden, thinks nothing of trouble, attempts what is above its strength, pleads no excuse of impossibility. It is therefore able to undertake all things, and it completes many things, and warrants them to take effect, where he who does not love would faint and lie down.

Though weary, it is not tired; though pressed, it is not straitened; though alarmed, it is not confounded; but as a living flame it forces itself upwards and securely passes through all.

Love is active and sincere, courageous, patient, faithful, prudent and manly.

From *The Imitation of Christ.*

Enjoy the World

THOMAS TRAHERNE
(English; c. 1636–74)

Your enjoyment of the world is never right till every morning you awake in heaven; see yourself in your Father's palace; and look upon the skies, the earth, and the air as celestial joys, having such a reverend esteem of all as if you were among the angels. The bride of a monarch in her husband's chamber hath no such causes of delight as you.

You never enjoy the world aright till the sea itself floweth in your veins, till you are clothed with the heavens, and crowned with the stars, and perceive yourself to be the sole heir of the whole world, and more than so, because men are in it who are every one sole heirs as well as you. Till you can sing and rejoice and delight in God, as misers do in gold, and kings in sceptres, you never enjoy the world.

Till your spirit filleth the whole world, and the stars are your jewels; till you are as familiar with the ways of God in all ages as with your walk and table; till you are intimately acquainted with that shady nothing out of which the world was made; till you love men so as to desire their happiness with a thirst equal to the zeal of your own; till you delight in God for being good to all: you never enjoy the world.

From *Centuries of Meditation*.

A New World

MARK TWAIN
(American; 1835–1910)

This…will be the mightiest day in the history of our lives, the holiest, and the most generous towards us both – for it makes of two fractional lives a whole; it gives to two purposeless lives a work, and doubles the strength of each whereby to perform it; it gives to two questioning natures a reason for living, and something to live for; it will give a new gladness to the sunshine, a new fragrance to the flowers, a new beauty to the earth, a new mystery to life…it will give a new revelation to love, a new depth to sorrow, a new impulse to worship. In that day the scales will fall from our eyes and we shall look upon a new world.

From a letter to his fiancée.

A Totality of Giving

W. H. VANSTONE
(British; 1923–99)

A person who loves holds nothing for himself: he reserves nothing as of right. That which he holds, he holds either on trust or as gift… When a person loves, all that is in their power is invested with a sense of purpose, as available for the other, or becomes a cause or occasion of gratitude, as received by gift from the other.

The falsity of love is exposed wherever any limit is set by the will of those who profess to love: wherever, by their will something is withheld. Therefore the authenticity of love must imply a totality of giving – that which we call the giving of self or self-giving. The self is the totality of what a person has and is: and it is no less that this that is offered or made available in love.

From *Love's Endeavour, Love's Expense.*

I Shall Love You until I Die

VOLTAIRE
(French; 1694–1778)

Sensual pleasure passes and vanishes in the twinkling of an eye, but the friendship between us, the mutual confidence, the delights of the heart, the enchantment of the soul, these things do not perish and can never be destroyed. I shall love you until I die.

From a letter to Mme Denis.

Love Is a Direction

SIMONE WEIL
(French; 1909–43)

Before all things, God is love. Before all things, God loves himself. This love, this friendship of God, is the Trinity. Between the terms united by this relation of divine love there is more than nearness; there is also infinite nearness or identity. But, resulting from the Creation, the Incarnation and the Passion, there is also infinite distance. The totality of space and the totality of time, interposing their immensity, put an infinite distance between God and God.

Lovers or friends desire two things. The one is to love each other so much that they enter into each other and only make one being. The other is to love each other so much that, having half the globe between them, their union will not be diminished in the slightest degree. All any human being desires here below is perfectly realized in God. We have all these impossible desires within us as a mark of our destination. The love between God and God, which in itself is God, is this bond of double virtue; the bond which unites two beings so closely that they are no longer distinguishable and really form a single unity, and the bond which stretches across distance and triumphs over infinite separation…It is only necessary to know that love is a direction and not a state of the soul.

From *Waiting on God*; translated from the French by Emma Craufurd.

I Give You My Hand

WALT WHITMAN
(American; 1819–92)

Listen! I will be honest with you,
I do not offer the old smooth prizes, but offer rough new prizes,
These are the days that must happen to you:
You shall not heap up what is called riches,
You shall scatter with lavish hand all that you earn or
Achieve…

Camerado, I give you my hand!
I give you my love more precious than money,
I give you myself before preaching or law;
Will you give me yourself? will you come travel with me?
Shall we stick by each other as long as we live?

From *Song Of the Open Road*.

We Two Boys Together Clinging

WALT WHITMAN
(American; 1819–92)

We two boys together clinging,
One the other never leaving,
Up and down the roads going, North and South excursions
    making,
Power enjoying, elbows stretching, fingers clutching,
Armed and fearless, eating, drinking, sleeping, loving,
No law less than ourselves owning, sailing, soldiering,
    thieving, threatening,
Misers, menials, priests alarming, air breathing, water
    drinking, on the turf or the sea-beach dancing,
Cities wrenching, ease scoring, statutes mocking, feebleness
    chasing,
Fulfilling our foray.

A Wedding Toast

RICHARD WILBUR
(American; 1921–   )

St. John tells how, at Cana's wedding-feast,
The water-pots poured wine in such amount
That by his sober count
There were a hundred gallons at the least.

It made no earthly sense, unless to show
How whatsoever love elects to bless
Brims to a sweet excess
That can without depletion overflow.

Which is to say that what love sees is true;
That the world's fullness is not made but found.
Life hungers to abound
And pour its plenty out for such as you.

Now, if your loves will lend an ear to mine,
I toast you both, good son and dear new daughter.
May you not lack for water,
And may that water smack of Cana's wine

Her Love Is My Life

WOODROW WILSON
(American; 1856–1924)

I've been reckoning up, in a tumultuous, heartful sort of way, the value of my…wife to me. I can't state the result – there are no terms of value in which it can be stated – but perhaps I can give you some idea of what its proportions would be if it were stated. She has taken all real pain out of my life: her wonderful loving sympathy exalts even my occasional moods of despondency into a sort or hallowed sadness out of which I come stronger and better. She has given to my ambitions a meaning, an assurance, and a purity which they never had before: with her by my side, ardently devoted to me and to my cause, understanding all my thoughts and all my aims, I feel that I can make the utmost of every power I possess. She has brought into my life the sunshine which was needed to keep it from growing stale and morbid: that has steadily been bringing back into my spirits their old gladness and boyhood, their old delight in play and laughter: – that sweetest sunshine of deep, womanly love, unfailing, gentle patience, even happy spirits, and spontaneous mirth, that is purest, swiftest tonic to a spirit prone to fret and apt to flag. She has given me that perfect rest of heart and mind of whose existence I had never so much as dreamed before she came to me, which springs out of assured oneness of hope and sympathy – and which, for me, means life and success. Above all she has given me herself to live for! Her arms are able to hold me up against the world: her eyes are able to charm away every care; her words are my solace and inspiration and all because her love is my life.

From a letter to his wife.

He Wishes for the Cloths of Heaven

W. B. YEATS
(Irish; 1865–1939)

Had I the heavens' embroidered cloths,
Enwrought with golden and silver light,
The blue and the dim and the dark cloths
Of night and light and the half-light,
I would spread the cloths under your feet:
But I, being poor, have only my dreams;
I have spread my dreams under your feet;
Tread softly because you tread on my dreams.

A Drinking Song

W. B. YEATS
(Irish; 1865–1939)

Wine comes in at the mouth
And love comes in at the eye;
That's all we know for truth
Before we grow old and die.
I lift the glass to my mouth,
I look at you, and I sigh.

Appendices

Perfect Hymns for Weddings

Most Christian wedding ceremonies include several hymns for con-
gregational singing. The usual custom is to sing the first hymn after
the welcome and opening remarks, a second after the exchange of
vows, and a third after the signing of the register; a fourth may be
sung at communion, if this forms part of the service.

The main points to consider when choosing hymns for a wedding
are as follows:

- Hymns or religious music of any kind cannot, by law, be included
  in a civil marriage ceremony. The following remarks therefore
  apply only to church weddings and blessings.

- Ideally, you should consider the words of your hymns with the
  same care that you would choose words to be read. The verses
  should reflect the joyful nature of the occasion and you should
  make sure that you feel comfortable with the beliefs and feelings
  expressed. Note that some very popular hymns may be quite inappropriate for use at a wedding (e.g. 'Fight the Good Fight').

- The simplest way to find hymns and check their words is probably
  to borrow one of the hymn books in regular use at the church in
  which you are getting married. Alternatively, there are now a range
  of websites that provide the words to hymns (some also supply an
  audio track). Be aware that the words given may vary significantly
  from one source to another, usually owing to attempts to modern-
  ize the language. Where this is the case, be clear about which version you prefer and – above all – make sure that everybody uses
  the same version on the day: it is not unknown for church choirs
  to find that the words on their music are different from those
  being sung by the congregation!

- As with readings, any hymns chosen must be approved by the offi-
  ciating priest or minister, whose decision is final. Although most
  ministers will try hard to meet your wishes, some have strong feelings about particular hymns or styles of music. Note also that

some hymns (or verses of hymns) may be considered inappropriate at certain times of the church year, such as Lent or Advent.

- If possible, arrange a meeting with the church organist or director of music. He or she will have a wide knowledge of the hymns that other couples have chosen and should be able to make many useful suggestions; he or she will also be able to remind you of the tunes.

- Because you want the hymns to sound rousing and joyful it is best to choose pieces that the congregation – some of whom may not have attended a church service for years – will know and enjoy singing. In practice, this means erring on the side of the traditional and familiar. If you are determined to go for more unusual choices, then you should arrange for the church choir (or a group of strong singers) to lead the congregation.

A list of some 40 of the most enduringly popular wedding hymns follows.

'All Creatures of Our God and King'
(traditional melody arranged by Ralph Vaughan Williams, words by William H. Draper after St Francis of Assissi)

'All My Hope on God Is Founded'
(music by Herbert Howells, words by Robert Bridges after Joachim Neander)

'All People that on Earth Do Dwell'
(traditional melody, words by William Kethe)

'All Things Bright and Beautiful'
(traditional melody, words by C. F. Alexander)

'Amazing Grace'
(traditional melody, words by John Newton)

'At the Name of Jesus'
(music by (i) W. H. Monk or (ii) Michael Brierly, words by Caroline Maria Noel)

'Be Still for the Presence of the Lord'
(music and words by David Evans)

'Be Thou My Vision'
(traditional melody, words adapted from the Irish by Mary E.
Byrne and Eleanor Hull)

'Breathe on Me, Breath of God'
(music by Charles Lockhart, words by Edwin Hatch)

'Come Down, O Love Divine'
(music by Ralph Vaughan Williams, words by Bianco da Siena
translated by R. F. Littledale)

'Crown Him with Many Crowns'
(music by George J. Elvey, words by Matthew Bridges)

'Dear Lord and Father of Mankind'
(music by Hubert Parry, words by John Greenleaf Whittier)

'Father, Lord of All Creation'
(music by Cyril Taylor, words by Stuart Cross)

'For the Beauty of the Earth'
(traditional melody arranged by Geoffrey Shaw, words by
Folliot S. Pierpoint)

'Give Me Joy in My Heart'
(traditional)

'Great Is Thy Faithfulness'
(music by William Runyon, words by Thomas Chisholm)

'Guide Me, O Thou Great Redeemer'
(music by John Hughes, words by William Williams translated
by Peter Williams)

'How Great Thou Art'
(traditional melody, words by Carl Boberg translated by Stuart
K. Hine)

'Immortal, Invisible, God Only Wise'
(traditional melody arranged by John Roberts, words by Walter Chalmers Smith)

'King of Glory, King of Peace'
(music by Joseph David Jones, words by George Herbert)

'Lead Us, Heavenly Father'
(music by Friedrich Filitz, words by James Edmeston)

'Let All the World in Every Corner Sing'
(music by Basil Harwood, words by George Herbert)

'Lord of All Hopefulness'
(traditional melody arranged by Martin Shaw, words by Jan Struther)

'Lord of the Dance'
(traditional melody, words by Sydney Carter)

'Love Divine, All Loves Excelling'
(music by John Stainer, words by Charles Wesley)

'Make Me a Channel of Your Peace'
(music by Sebastian Temple, words attributed to St Francis of Assissi)

'Morning Has Broken'
(traditional melody, words by Eleanor Farjeon)

'Now Thank We All Our God'
(music by Johann Crüger, words by Martin Rinkart translated by Catherine Winkworth)

'O Jesus I Have Promised'
(music by Arthur H. Mann, words by John E. Bode)

'O Perfect Love, All Human Thought Transcending'
(music by John B. Dykes, words by Dorothy Frances Gurney)

'O Worship the King'
(music by William Croft, words by Robert Grant)

'Praise My Soul the King of Heaven'
(music by John Goss, words by Henry Francis Lyte)

'Praise to the Lord, the Almighty'
(traditional melody, words by Joachim Neander translated by
Catherine Winkworth)

'Shine, Jesus Shine'
(music and words by Graham Kendrick)

'Tell Out My Soul'
(music by Walter Greatorex, words by Timothy Dudley-Smith)

'The King of Love My Shepherd Is'
(music by John B. Dykes, words by Henry Williams Baker)

'The Lord's My Shepherd'
(music by Jessie Seymour Irvine, words from the Scottish
Psalter)

'Thine Be the Glory'
(music adapted from G. F. Handel, words by Edmund Louis
Budry translated by Richard Birch Hoyle)

'This Little Light of Mine'
(traditional)

'To God Be the Glory'
(music by William H. Doane, words by Fanny J. Crosby)

Short Quotes

In every marriage more than a week old, there are grounds for divorce. The trick is to find, and continue to find, grounds for marriage.

Robert Anderson (1917–   )

Success in marriage is much more than finding the right person: it is a matter of being the right person.

Anonymous

A man admitting he is wrong is wise. A man admitting he is wrong when he is right is married.

Anonymous

The cure for love is marriage, and the cure for marriage is love again.

Anonymous

If it weren't for marriage, men would spend all their lives thinking they had no faults at all.

Anonymous

I married beneath me. All women do.

Nancy Astor (1879–1964)

Like everything which is not the involuntary result of fleeting emotion but the creation of time and will, any marriage, happy or unhappy, is infinitely more interesting than any romance, however passionate.

W. H. Auden (1907–73)

A man finds himself seven years older the day after his marriage.

Francis Bacon (1561–1626)

A woman must be a genius to create a good husband.

Honoré de Balzac (1799–1850)

Marriage is our last, best chance to grow up.

Joseph Barth (20th century)

All weddings are similar, but every marriage is different.

John Berger (1926–)

Marriage is not just spiritual communion, it is also remembering to take out the trash.

Joyce Brothers (1928–)

If variety is the spice of life, marriage is the big can of leftover Spam.

Johnny Carson (1925–2005)

My most brilliant achievement was my ability to be able to persuade my wife to marry me.

Sir Winston Churchill (1874–1965)

Marriage is a wonderful invention; but then again, so is a bicycle repair kit.

Billy Connolly (1942–)

Never go to bed mad. Stay up and fight.

Phyllis Diller (1917–)

It destroys one's nerves to be amiable every day to the same human being.

Benjamin Disraeli (1804–81)

The reason husbands and wives do not understand each other is because they belong to different sexes.

Dorothy Dix (1861–1951)

There's only one way to have a happy marriage and as soon as I learn what it is I'll get married again.

Clint Eastwood (1930–)

A man in love is incomplete until he has married. Then he's finished.

Zsa Zsa Gabor (1917–)

I first learned the concepts of non-violence in my marriage.

Mahatma Gandhi (1869–1948)

Love is an ideal thing, marriage a real thing; a confusion of the real with the ideal never goes unpunished.

Johann Wolfgang von Goethe (1749–1832)

The others were only my wives, but you, my dear, will be my widow.

Sacha Guitry (1885–1957)

I should like to see any kind of a man, distinguishable from a gorilla, that some good and even pretty woman could not shape a husband out of.

Oliver Wendell Holmes (1809–94)

There is nothing nobler or more admirable than when two people who see eye to eye keep house as man and wife, confounding their enemies and delighting their friends.

Homer (8th century BC)

Only two things are necessary to keep one's wife happy. One is to let her think she is having her own way – the other, to let her have it.

Lyndon B. Johnson (1908–73)

Love is blind, but marriage restores its sight.

Georg Christoph Lichtenberg (1742–99)

The men that women marry,
And why they marry them, will always be
A marvel and a mystery to the world.

Henry Wadsworth Longfellow (1807–82)

A successful marriage requires falling in love many times, always with the same person.

Mignon McLaughlin (1913–83)

One doesn't have to get anywhere in a marriage. It's not a public conveyance.

Iris Murdoch (1919–99)

To keep your marriage brimming,
With love in the loving cup,
Whenever you're wrong, admit it;
Whenever you're right, shut up.

Ogden Nash (1902–71)

It is not a lack of love, but a lack of friendship that makes unhappy marriages.

Friedrich Nietzsche (1844–1900)

Love is no assignment for cowards.

Ovid (43 BC–17 AD)

A good marriage is that in which each appoints the other guardian of his solitude.

Rainer Maria Rilke (1875–1926)

Always get married early in the morning. That way, if it doesn't work out, you haven't wasted a whole day.

Mickey Rooney (1920–   )

Never feel remorse for what you have thought about your wife; she has thought much worse things about you.

Jean Rostand (1894–1977)

Before marriage, a man will lie awake thinking about something you said; after marriage, he'll fall asleep before you finish saying it.

Helen Rowland (1875–1950)

I love being married. It's so great to find that one special person you want to annoy for the rest of your life.

Rita Rudner (1956–)

Even in civilized mankind faint traces of monogamous instinct can be perceived.

Bertrand Russell (1872–1970)

Love does not consist in gazing at each other, but in looking outward in the same direction.

Antoine de Saint-Exupéry (1900–44)

Chains do not hold a marriage together. It is threads, hundreds of tiny threads, which sew people together through the years.

Simone Signoret (1921–85)

My advice to you is to get married. If you find a good wife, you'll be happy; if not, you'll become a philosopher.

Socrates (c. 470–399 BC)

No woman should marry a teetotaller, or a man who does not smoke.

Robert Louis Stevenson (1850–94)

A lady of 47 who has been married 27 years and has 6 children knows what love really is and once described it for me like this: 'Love is what you've been through with somebody'.

James Thurber (1894–1961)

What counts in making a happy marriage is not how compatible you are, but how you deal with incompatibility.

Leo Tolstoy (1828–1910)

Love seems the swiftest, but it is the slowest of all growths. No man or woman really knows what perfect love is until they have been married a quarter of a century.

Mark Twain (1835–1910)

Marriage is the only adventure open to the cowardly.

Voltaire (1694–1778)

Love conquers everything except poverty and toothache.

Mae West (1893–1980)

Men marry because they are tired; women because they are curious. Both are disappointed.

Oscar Wilde (1854–1900)

All the unhappy marriages come from the husbands having brains. What good are brains to a man? They only unsettle him.

P. G. Wodehouse (1881–1975)

Acknowledgements

The editor and publisher are grateful to those listed below for permission to reprint copyright material. While every effort has been made to trace and contact all copyright holders, in a few cases this proved impossible at the time of going to press. The publisher will be grateful to be informed of any errors or omissions in the details given below, so that these can be rectified in any future reprint or edition.

Bible: Extracts from the Authorized Version of the Bible (The King James Bible), the rights in which are vested in the Crown, are reproduced by permission of the Crown's Patentee, Cambridge University Press. Extracts from the New Revised Standard Version (Anglicized Edition) of the Bible are copyright © 1989, 1995 and used by permission of the Division of Christian Education of the National Council of the Churches of Christ in the USA.

Dannie Abse: 'Epithalamion' from *New and Collected Poems* (Hutchinson, 2003); reprinted by permission of The Random House Group Ltd.

Diane Ackerman: extract from *A Natural History of Love* (Random House USA, 1994); copyright © Diane Ackerman and reprinted by permission of Random House, Inc.

Daisy Ashford: extract from *The Young Visiters* (Chatto & Windus, 1951); reprinted by permission of the Random House Group Ltd.

Margaret Atwood: 'Habitation' from *Procedures for Underground* (OUP, 1971); copyright © 1970 Margaret Atwood and 1990 Oxford University Press Canada; reprinted by permission of Curtis Brown Group Ltd, London and Oxford University Press.

W. H. Auden: 'Carry Her Over the Water' from *Collected Poems* (Faber & Faber, 1976); reprinted by permission of Faber & Faber.

Michael Blumenthal: 'A Marriage' from *Against Romance* (Viking Penguin, 1987); copyright © Michael Blumenthal.

Robert Bly: 'Such Different Wants' from *Loving A Woman in Two Worlds* (Doubleday, 1985); copyright © Robert Bly and reprinted by permission of Doubleday, a division of Random House, Inc.

Raymond Carver: 'Late Fragment' from *All of Us: The Collected Poems* (Harvill Press, 1996); reprinted by permission of the Random House Group Ltd.

Kate Clanchy: 'For a Wedding' and 'Patagonia' from *Slattern* (Picador, 2001); copyright © 2001 Kate Clanchy and reprinted by permission of Macmillan Publishers Ltd.

Wendy Cope: 'Giving up Smoking' from *If I Don't Know* (Faber & Faber, 2001); reprinted by permission of Faber & Faber.

Louise Cuddon: 'I'll Be There'; copyright © Louise Cuddon and reprinted by kind permission of Jonathan Clowes Ltd., London, on behalf of Julia Watson.

Louis de Bernières: extract from *Captain Corelli's Mandolin* (Vintage, 1995); reprinted by permission of The Random House Group Ltd.

Michael Donaghy: 'The Present' from *Dances Learned Last Night: Poems 1975–1995* (Picador, 2000); copyright © 2000 Michael Donaghy and reprinted by permission of Macmillan Publishers Ltd.

Carol Ann Duffy: 'Valentine' from *Mean Time* (Anvil Press Poetry, 1993): 'White Writing' from *Feminine Gospels* (Picador, 2002); copyright © 2002 Carol Ann Duffy and reprinted by permission of Macmillan Publishers Ltd.

T. S. Eliot: 'A Dedication to My Wife' from *The Complete Poems and Plays* (Faber & Faber, 1978); reprinted by permission of Faber & Faber.

U. A. Fanthorpe: 'Atlas' and '7301' from *Collected Poems 1978–2003* (Peterloo Poets, 2005); reprinted by permission of Peterloo Poets.

James Fenton: 'Hinterhof'; copyright © 1993 James Fenton and reprinted by permission of PFD on behalf of James Fenton.

Erich Fried: 'What It Is' from *Love Poems* (Calder Publications, 1991); translation by Stuart Hood, copyright © the Calder Educational Trust.

Gloria Fuertes: 'When I Hear Your Name' from *Off the Map* (Wesleyan University Press, 1984); translation copyright © 1984 Philip Levine and Ada Long and reprinted by permission of Wesleyan University Press.

Robert Graves: 'A Slice of Wedding Cake' from *Complete Poems in One Volume* (Carcanet, 2000); reprinted by permission of Carcanet Press Ltd.

Sophie Hannah: 'Match' from *First of the Last Chances* (Carcanet, 2003); reprinted by permission of Carcanet Press Ltd.

Adrian Henri: 'Love Is' from *Collected Poems* (Alison & Busby, 1986); copyright © 1986 Adrian Henri and reprinted by permission of the estate of Adrian Henri c/o Rogers, Coleridge & White Ltd., 20 Powis Mews, London W11 1JN.

Jane Holland: 'They Are a Tableau at the Kissing Gate' from *The Brief History of a Disreputable Woman* (Bloodaxe, 1997); reprinted by permission of Jane Holland.

Michael Ignatieff: extract from 'Lodged in the Heart and Memory' (*Times Literary Supplement*, 15 April 1988); reprinted by permission of A P Watt Ltd on behalf of Michael Ignatieff.

Elizabeth Jennings: 'Tell Me' and 'Friendship' from *New Collected Poems* (Carcanet, 2002); reprinted by permission of David Highham Associates Ltd.

Juan Ramon Jiménez: 'When, With You Asleep'; translation copyright © 1986 Perry Higman and reprinted by permission of City Lights Books.

Jenny Joseph: 'The Sun Has Burst the Sky' from *Selected Poems* (Bloodaxe, 1992); copyright © Jenny Joseph and reprinted by permission of Johnson & Alcock Ltd.

James Laughlin: 'I Want To Breathe' from *Selected Poems 1935-1985* (City Lights Books, 1986); copyright © 1986 James Laughlin and reprinted by permission of New Directions Publishing Corp.

Dorianne Laux: 'Kissing' from *What We Carry* (BOA Editions, 1994); copyright © 1994 Dorianne Laux and reprinted by permission of BOA Editions, Ltd.,

Anne Morrow Lindbergh: extract from *Gift from the Sea* (Chatto & Windus, 1955); copyright © 1955, 1975, renewed 1983 Anne Morrow Lindbergh; reprinted by permission of The Random House Group Ltd and Pantheon Books, a division of Random House, Inc.

Christopher Logue: 'Poem' from *Selected Poems* (Faber & Faber, 1996); reprinted by permission of Faber & Faber.

Norman MacCaig: 'Sure Proof' and 'True Ways of Knowing' from *The Poems of Norman MacCaig* (Polygon, 2005); reprinted by permission of Polygon, an imprint of Birlinn Ltd (www.birlinn.co.uk).

John Masefield: 'Being Her Friend' from *Poems* (Macmillan, 1951); reprinted by permission of the Society of Authors as the literary representative of the estate of John Masefield.

Peter Meinke: 'The First Marriage' from *Scars* (University of Pittsburgh Press, 1996); copyright © 1996 and reprinted by permission of the University of Pittsburgh Press.

Edwin Muir: 'The Confirmation' and 'Song' from *Collected Poems* (Faber & Faber, 1960); reprinted by permission of Faber & Faber.

Ogden Nash: 'The Strange Case of Mr. Ormantude's Bride' copyright © 1942 Ogden Nash and reprinted by permission of Curtis Brown, Ltd: 'I Do, I Will, I Have' from *Candy Is Dandy: The Best of Ogden Nash* (André Deutsch, 1994); copyright © 1948 Ogden Nash and reprinted by permission of the Carlton Publishing Group and Curtis Brown, Ltd.

John Ormond: 'In September' from *Selected Poems* (Seren Books, 1995); reprinted by permission of Seren Books and the Estate of John Ormond.

Alice Oswald: 'Wedding' from *The Thing in the Gap-Stone Stile* (Oxford University Press, 1996); copyright © Alice Oswald and reprinted by PFD on behalf of Alice Oswald.

Brian Patten: 'Her Song' and 'When You Wake Tomorrow' from *Love Poems* (Allen & Unwin, 1981); copyright © 1981 Brian Patten; reprinted by permission of HarperCollins Publishers Ltd.

Kathleen Raine: 'Amo Ergo Sum' from *The Collected Poems of Kathleen Raine* (Golgonooza Press, 2000); copyright © 2000 Kathleen Raine and reprinted by permission of the Estate of Kathleen Raine.

Rainer Maria Rilke: extracts from *Letters to a Young Poet* (Random House USA, 2001); translation copyright © 1984 Stephen Mitchell and reprinted by permission of Random House, Inc.

Jalal al-din Rumi: 'Quatrain' from *The Essential Rumi* (HarperCollins, 1997); translation copyright © Coleman Barks: 'The Taste of Morning' from *The Glance: Songs of Soul-Meeting* (Viking Penguin, 1999); translation copyright © Coleman Barks.

Bertrand Russell: extract from *Marriage and Morals* (Allen & Unwin, 1930); copyright © The Bertrand Russell Peace Foundation and Taylor & Francis Ltd.

Vernon Scannell: 'A Love Song' from *Of Love and War: New and Selected Poems* (Robson Books, 2002); reprinted by permission of Vernon Scannell.

E. J. Scovell: 'A Betrothal' from *Collected Poems* (Carcanet, 1988); reprinted by permission of Carcanet Press Ltd.

Wisława Szymborska: 'True Love' from *View With a Grain of Sand* (Faber & Faber, 1996); translation by Stanisław Barańczak and Clare Cavanagh, reprinted by permission of Faber & Faber.

A. S. J. Tessimond: 'Not Love Perhaps' from *Collected Poems, with Translations from Jacques Prevert* (Whiteknights Press, 1993); reprinted by permission of the University of Reading.

W. H. Vanstone: extract from *Love's Endeavour, Love's Expense* (Darton, Longman & Todd, 1977); reprinted by permission of Darton, Longman & Todd.

Simone Weil: extract from *Waiting on God*, translated by Emma Crauford (Routledge & Kegan Paul, 1951); reprinted by permission of Taylor & Francis Ltd.

Richard Wilbur: 'A Wedding Toast' from *The Mind-Reader* (Faber & Faber, 1977); reprinted by permission of Faber & Faber.

W. B. Yeats: 'He Wishes for the Cloths of Heaven' and 'A Drinking Song' from *Collected Poems* (Macmillan, 1950); reprinted by permission of A P Watt Ltd on behalf of Gráinne Yeats.

Index

The following is an index of (i) the *titles* of works cited and (ii) the first lines of the readings as printed. Editorial titles supplied for prose extracts have not generally been indexed. The items appear in strict alphabetical order.